RESEARCH COMPANION TO GREEN INTERNATIONAL MANAGEMENT STUDIES

Research Companion to Green International Management Studies

A Guide for Future Research, Collaboration and Review Writing

Edited by

Deborah E. de Lange

Suffolk University, Boston, MA, USA

Edward Elgar
Cheltenham, UK • Northampton, MA, USA

Published by
Edward Elgar Publishing Limited
The Lypiatts
15 Lansdown Road
Cheltenham
Glos GL50 2JA
UK

Edward Elgar Publishing, Inc.
William Pratt House
9 Dewey Court
Northampton
Massachusetts 01060
USA

A catalogue record for this book
is available from the British Library

Library of Congress Control Number: 2010926007

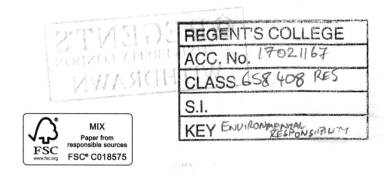

ISBN 978 1 84980 363 2 (cased)

Printed and bound by MPG Books Group, UK

Contents

Contributors

Bobby Banerjee is Professor of Management and Associate Dean (Research) at the College of Business, University of Western Sydney. He has a tendency to write a bit and has published some articles in journals. His research interests include sustainability, corporate social responsibility [sic], indigenous ecology, post-colonialism, cultural studies, climate justice, translocalism. He is currently working on a book provisionally titled *Why the Human Race Should Not be Allowed to Exist*.

Oana Branzei (facilitator) is Assistant Professor of Strategy at the Richard Ivey School of Business at the University of Western Ontario. As an academic, teacher and consultant, Oana enables executives and students to successfully transform local and global tensions among economic, social and environmental sustainability into future sources of competitiveness. Her current research initiatives explore the origins and processes of sustainable advantage, the formation of path-breaking strategies and capabilities and the creation and diffusion of pro-poor, for-profit business models.

Amanda Bullough is an Assistant Professor of Global Entrepreneurship at Thunderbird School of Global Management, Arizona, USA. Dr Bullough teaches the new social entrepreneurship course at Thunderbird and has previously taught graduate- and undergraduate-level entrepreneurship, management and international business courses. Dr Bullough has presented on leadership and entrepreneurship at numerous international business and management conferences and has written a number of papers on entrepreneurship, women in entrepreneurship and leadership, and cross-cultural leadership, mostly for the purposes of the advancement of women in business and economic development.

Timo Busch, PhD is working as Senior Researcher at the Swiss Federal Institute of Technology (ETH) in Zurich, Switzerland. His research interests include corporate strategies towards a low carbon economy, organizational adaptation to climate change and the business case of corporate environmental sustainability. He teaches at ETH and FU Berlin on courses on corporate sustainability and strategy. Before joining ETH Timo worked at the Wuppertal Institute for Climate, Environment and Energy in Germany, focusing on corporate eco-efficiency, sustainable finance and climate change.

Dan V. Caprar (facilitator) is a lecturer at the Australian School of Business, University of New South Wales, in Sydney, Australia. He received his MBA and a PhD from the University of Iowa in the United States, and has also worked and lived in the United Kingdom and Romania. In his research, Dan addresses questions related to the inter-actions between business and the broader societal context, with particular interest in cross-cultural aspects; given his consulting experience, Dan is also interested in understanding and bridging the gap between academics and practitioners.

Tom Cooper, PhD is an Assistant Professor at Memorial University of Newfoundland in Canada. Tom has been a researcher, consultant and advisor in the corporate responsibility and business ethics field for over 17 years. He spent over seven years as a Senior Manager at PricewaterhouseCoopers UK consulting practice and currently researches the link between corporate responsibility, business ethics and risk management.

Deborah E. de Lange (editor, contributor and facilitator) is an Assistant Professor of Strategy and International Business at the Sawyer Business School, Suffolk University in Boston, USA. Dr de Lange obtained her PhD at the University of Toronto and will be publishing her PhD disser-tation as a book entitled, *Power and Influence: The Embeddedness of Nations*. Aside from sustainability, her research interests include trade, foreign direct investment, diplomacy, international business and organiza-tions, corporate governance and network and embeddedness theories. She currently teaches globalization and sustainable strategy at Suffolk and has taught high-technology strategy at the University of Toronto.

Mary S. Finney received her PhD in Organizational Behavior/Organizational Development at Case Western Reserve University, Cleveland, Ohio. She is a faculty member in the College of Business at Ohio University, Athens, Ohio. Her research focuses on global leadership, organizational design and innovation for 'going green', organizational change and development, international collaboration and partnership development and business as an agent of world benefit. Her consulting in the United States, Africa, India, Brazil and Europe with business, non-profit, governmental and educational institutions focuses on organizational change and develop-ment, sustainability, entrepreneurship, team, leadership, collaboration and inter-organizational partnership development.

Jijun Gao is an Assistant Professor at the Asper School of Business, University of Manitoba. He received his PhD from the Richard Ivey

School of Business of the University of Western Ontario. Dr Gao focuses his research on corporate social responsibility, business sustainability and competitive strategy. Recently he has been exploring the interaction between corporate social responsibility and social irresponsibility.

C. Gopinath (PhD, University of Massachusetts Amherst) is Associate Professor, Sawyer Business School, Suffolk University, Boston, MA. His research, teaching and consulting span the areas of strategy and international business. His current areas of interest include globalization and indigenous management.

Olga Hawn was born in Russia and received a BA in Economics and an MA in International Business from Plekhanov Russian Academy of Economics. She then travelled to the UK to obtain an MSc in Management Research from Said Business School at Oxford University. At the moment Olga is pursuing a PhD in Strategy at Duke University's Fuqua School of Business in the United States; her research interests include corporate social responsibility, social entrepreneurship and sustainability.

Elvira Haezendonck (PhD, 2001, Vrije Universiteit Brussel and Solvay Business School) is Assistant Professor at the University of Brussels (VUB) and at the University of Antwerp. Her research covers various topics in the field of management, strategy and policy: environmental strategy, competition analysis and stakeholder management. She teaches courses on management, competition strategy, port management and strategy and corporate social responsibility, mostly at Masters level, and has been Guest Lecturer at the University of Rotterdam (MEL) since 2005 and at EUROMED Marseille (Maritime MBA) since 2007. Since 2010 she holds a Research Chair on public–private partnerships at VUB. She has published various articles, books and book chapters in these domains, with a recent (2007) Edward Elgar book publication, *Transport Project Evaluation*. Since 1998, she has been involved in over 30 national and EU research projects on, for example, long-term strategy analyses, multinational strategies and impact assessments.

Dean Hennessy is an Assistant Professor of Organization and Strategy, and Fellow of the Center for Innovation Research (CIR) at Tilburg University, the Netherlands.

Laurie Ingraham is currently a PhD student at the University of Calgary, Canada, where her research focus is carbon capture and storage and cluster development. Her other degrees include a Masters in Social Work and a Masters of Science in Management. During her 15 years as a business owner of a consulting group, she was also an international speaker.

Mai Skott Linneberg is Assistant Professor at the Aarhus School of Business, Aarhus University, Denmark. In her doctoral dissertation (published 2008) she analyzed standardization and rule-making of organic agriculture in Denmark and Sweden from an organizational and governance perspective. She has published articles in *NOS* and *International Journal of Public Policy* and several book chapters.

Daina Mazutis is a doctoral candidate at the Richard Ivey School of Business (UWO) and her research focuses on the strategic leadership of corporate social strategies. In addition to numerous awards received in both her MBA and undergraduate degrees, Daina is currently a Trudeau Scholar and SSHRC doctoral fellow. She has published in *Management Learning, Business Horizons, AOM* and *ASAC Best Paper* proceedings as well as presented extensively at international conferences. Prior to her doctoral studies, Daina enjoyed a successful career in advertising, marketing and sales, specializing in the strategic planning, research, development and implementation of national marketing campaigns.

Jonatan Pinkse is Assistant Professor at the Universiteit van Amsterdam Business School, the Netherlands. His research deals with business responses to climate change and sustainability. He has published papers in various international journals, including *Journal of International Business Studies, California Management Review* and *Business & Society*, and has co-authored *International Business and Global Climate Change* published by Routledge (2009), as well as chapter contributions to various books.

Claire A. Simmers (facilitator), PhD, is a Professor of Management and department chair at Saint Joseph's University in Philadelphia, PA. She has been at SJU for the past 14 years and she received her PhD from Drexel University, Philadelphia in strategic management. Her current research interests are in the sociotechnical interfaces in the Internet-connected workplace, including the changing workplace, human capital contributions to competitive advantage and strategic decision-making.

Natalie Slawinski is an Assistant Professor of Strategic Management at Memorial University of Newfoundland's Faculty of Business. Her research examines the role of organizational time orientation in shaping organizational responses to social and environmental issues. She has carried out research on responses to climate change in the oil and gas industry. She received her PhD from the Richard Ivey Business School in London, Ontario.

Josephine Stomp is an Assistant Professor at the Odette School of Business, Windsor, Canada. She completed her PhD on resistance to change amongst US auto industry elites at the Schulich School of Business, Toronto, Canada. Her research interests are sources of resistance and change in hegemonic fields as a result of shifts in field membership and social values. This includes the role of business elites, such as the Big 3 and Business Roundtable, and competing business models, such as competition versus collaboration and shareholder versus stakeholder interests, from the perspective of institutional theory.

Svenja Tams is Lecturer of Organization Studies at the University of Bath, School of Management, UK. Her doctoral research at London Business School examined self-directed and constructivist approaches to learning in organizations. Her current research examines careers, leadership and learning in response to contemporary challenges of global society.

Patricia Gonçalves Vidal (facilitator) is an Assistant Professor at Universidade Presbiteriana Mackenzie, in São Paulo, Brazil. She graduated in Economics from the Federal University of Rio de Janeiro (1989), and received a Masters degree in Production Engineering from COPPE/UFRJ, Rio de Janeiro (1993) and a Doctor of Business Administration (DBA) from Boston University (2003). She has been researching the following topics: decision-making, organizational learning and the learning curve.

Diana J. Wong-MingJi (Workshop participant) is an Associate Professor in Strategy and Entrepreneurship at Eastern Michigan University. Her engagement in economic development with NGOs and non-profit organizations extends from a global to a local scope. She works on issues related to international trade, women, homelessness and ecological systems of entrepreneurship.

Susan L. Young is a PhD candidate at the Ohio State University. Her research interests include international business, corporate social responsibility and entrepreneurship. She is currently working on her dissertation, which examines institutional influences on CSR behavior across countries, and has made chapter contributions to various books, most recently on opportunity formation and the implications for the field of entrepreneurship.

Acknowledgments

In addition to thanking all the listed participants in this compendium for being involved in this endeavor and completing such high-quality work, many who I consider friends, I would also like to highlight the contributions made by a couple of people. At its inception, my good friends Natalie Slawinski and Dan Caprar supported the idea of the Professional Development Workshop at the Academy of Management conference in Chicago 2009, which is the basis of this work. They freely offered their ideas as the workshop proposal came to shape. I would also like to thank Olav Sorenson for his early comments when it seemed I was designing a mini-conference. Yes, it became a smaller version of the original ambitious plan. Thanks also go to Prescott Ensign and Andy Hoffman for publishing advice. I'd also like to thank Judith Walls for PhD-level reading recommendations. Also, many thanks go to Alan Sturmer, Senior Acquisitions Editor at Edward Elgar Publishing Ltd for accepting this manuscript for publication and for support throughout the process. Finally, I would like to wholeheartedly thank the Academy of Management conference division sponsors who took time to review and choose the workshop so that this work could be produced; they allowed us to have time and space at the conference: SIM the primary sponsor, and ONE, IM, BPS, OMT, PNP, OB, ODC, ITC, TIM, HR and PTC.

Sincerely,
Debbie de Lange, PhD

Preface
Deborah E. de Lange

This set of reviews is the intended result of a Professional Development Workshop (PDW) held at the Academy of Management 2009 conference in Chicago, entitled, 'Future Research Paths for Green International Management Studies'. I organized the participants into four groups, representing areas of interest related to sustainability: Corporate Social Responsibility; NGOs, IGOs, Government and Sustainability in Developing Nations; Environmental Innovation and Talent; and Academic Theory. The first three subfields are phenomena-centered and the fourth group ties the broader field of sustainability together from a theoretical perspective. The latter group's purpose was to summarize the theories it found prevalent in the sustainability literature and make suggestions regarding which theory(ies) may be most promising for future sustainability research.

Prior to the conference meeting, participants who volunteered to be involved, based on their interests, chose for review three high-quality academic journal articles related to one of the subfields. The reviews were completed before the meeting so that all participants could read all the reviews. At the PDW meeting, the groups discussed what they found in common based on their reviews so that they could make summary recommendations as to where future research in their subfield should go. They were to first examine the current state of the literature, next, to find gaps in it, and following this, make future research recommendations. The overviews at the beginning of each section of reviews in this book were written after these discussions to capture them. They present some main ideas for area guidance.

The set-up of this PDW is instructive for other areas; the same framework and set-up, organizing many people to research the current state of a field may be replicated; other areas will need the same review and consolidated direction for future research. It's also a way for those who are interested in an area to bring themselves up to speed very quickly in a field; no previous knowledge is required, just a willingness to contribute some reviews. However, most of the participants in this PDW were dedicated experts. Another advantage is that this approach promotes an emerging field, precisely by getting a wide range of people together – from those who are already experts to those who are interested.

Why read the result of this group's work? While admittedly not covering everything, it is a large compendium summarizing and reviewing many excellent articles in the field. Broad themes are outlined, suggesting opportunities for future research and the critiques by the participant authors provide valuable insights. They also refer to other articles not reviewed, integrating literature that someone reading the reviews can refer to for further reading. It's a wonderful springboard for researchers who are searching for inspiration and a quick way to help decide which articles to read. Many of the participants are focused researchers in this area and have already conveniently narrowed down the choices. Also interesting to note is that the reviews combine the views of a very diverse international group of scholars. Additionally, it makes excellent PhD-level course material. Whether it's for a course in sustainability, a related area, or a demonstration of how to critique articles, scholars will find this helpful in guiding their students. Mentors may ask their PhD students to review articles listed in the book and then reflect on what the authors in this book have to say as a comparison and point of discussion – excellent review practice.

Also, practitioners who intend to be leaders in their field will refer to this book. Rather than struggling to read many academic articles without the requisite training, they can learn about the latest ideas and learn about the debates. Consultants may read it and be thought leaders, sharing the ideas with their client managers. Corporate leaders and top managers in firms who want to obtain the big strategic picture will also gain insight; a competitive advantage is gained when the firm is set on the right track.

Each subfield offers some interesting themes and research opportunities to ponder, currently existing in the research and for future work. The Corporate Social Responsibility group (CSR), facilitated by Oana Branzei and Patricia Vidal, tells us that there are four main themes it can use to identify gaps; it is a holistic approach to explaining how the field may move forward. It suggests that researchers may address gaps by experimenting with other theories and approaches such as institutional theory and the use of narratives. Qualitative research is a popular suggestion amongst the researcher participants, in general. Searching for ways to make CSR, as a substantive and not ceremonial change, part of the manager's normal repertoire is a practical concern; the researchers' direction reflects grounded views – they want to discover how we can align interests so as to make real change. Perhaps, refining CSR concepts so as to develop a common language that all parties can understand may help them to communicate clearly and align interests.

The main purpose of the subfield, NGOs, IGOs, Government and Sustainability in Developing Nations, is to examine how various international actors and governments influence and promote sustainable practices by firms in developing nations. The group, facilitated by me, discussed the problem and opportunity of this being a multidisciplinary field including, but not limited to: political science, development, sustainability, strategy and organizations fields. This presents challenges for integration when, for example, definitions, such as that for sustainability, are not uniformly agreed upon. Also, dominant theories used in sustainability are the resource-based view and stakeholder theory, but given the level of analysis – international and related organizations – the researcher participants see an opportunity for testing and application of other theories such as institutional theory, as did the first group. Moreover, research has found it convenient to study the Triad nations whereas developing nations have not received much attention. Thus, this is an area ripe for future research.

The title of the third subfield, Environmental Innovation and Talent, is meant to group research relating to firms that adopt and develop environmental innovation; this must include the challenge of finding talented human resources to work on environmental innovation. The subfield group, facilitated by Claire Simmers, discovered many questions to ask and, as an example, wonders what drives firms to adopt environmental innovations. In addition to questions about firms and how they may attract/develop employees, the group recognized the environment – stakeholders – as an important influence on firm innovation. Theory development at the firm level is scarce and the group has identified a currently economic orientation to explanations for innovation in firms. Also, similar to the other subfields, definitions and measurement of seemingly the most basic of constructs – even environmental innovation – are deterring the field's inquiry. At the human resource level, more work has been undertaken, using leadership and core competence theories.

Finally, the mandate of the Academic Theory group, facilitated by Dan Caprar, was to examine all papers reviewed in order to prompt discussion about which theories are being used in the sustainability literature and to think about which theories make most sense to use in research going forward. Also, the area of sustainability may be one that is opportune for testing some theories more so than others. This is a big task and the expectation was that it would start a valuable discussion rather than come to solid conclusions. As we know, the field of organizational theory, the area from which most theories in use are derived, is multi-theoretical and while it has discussions about which theory should be of focus, no lasting conclusions have been or are expected to be reached. This group finds that most organizational theories are being used in sustainability studies; for example, a dominant theory is the resource-based view at the firm level, as was found by other groups. The group debated whether a new theory for the field is needed and did not come to a clear conclusion. However, it valued the contradictions in sustainability theorizing as opportunities, not barriers.

The participants did a tremendous amount of work and had lively discussions to reach a higher understanding of and to make recommendations for useful future research in an exciting emerging field that is critical at this time in the world's history and will be for generations to come; we have to make permanent behavioral changes and our organizations – whether firms, governments, or international organizations – are places of great influence. I believe that all my colleagues in this endeavor will agree that change is a main motivation for coming together to examine this academic field that has such great potential to make an impact on a world clearly in trouble and in need of solutions – today.

1 Writing a professional academic article review
Deborah E. de Lange

A professional review is different from those we learn to do at earlier stages of our academic training. Early on, PhDs are learning how to wade through the complications of the research. Most PhD programs train academics to critique articles in the area in which they are building their expertise. The approach may be more or less structured and is often unwritten and practiced in PhD seminars through discussion. The approaches are similar because they are ultimately teaching students not only to become good reviewers, but also to know what the ingredients and structure of the quality research articles are that they will be expected to produce. So, while they usually informally discuss and may write rough note critiques, the reviews are almost never written for an audience in a professional manner. Book reviews are usually found in academic journals and they are the best available examples of what a professional review looks like, but books are different from articles.

So, when I asked the contributors to this compendium to produce reviews, I asked them to include the components of a research article critique and gave them example book reviews to suggest that they write their journal article reviews to be interesting to an audience based on the style of the book reviews. After all, they would all need to read each others' reviews in order to review a great deal of literature in a short period of time and come to consensus about where the field is, what research gaps exist and to make recommendations for future research. Good article reviews were critical for this corroborative task.

This research companion contains professional-style critiques of journal articles, rather than books, because it is journal articles that tend to be the basis for the field of management. However, many important and seminal contributions have been made in book form, usually from fields such as sociology, social psychology and political science that are making crossover contributions to the field of management. A core academic expertise is critical review of journal articles. Reviews are published here to support the contributors' consensus regarding where the green international management field should go, to provide a quicker review of the available literature chosen by scholars in the field and to codify instructional material regarding critical review. In general, the review work of PhDs and journal reviewers is very much lost because no examples are published; how to review well becomes tacit rather than codified knowledge only because no one has thought to publish example reviews. Thus, this research companion is a guide for researchers and is also a source to improve the quality and consistency of PhD education. Moreover, it takes this a step further by demonstrating professional quality review writing.

IN-DEPTH ANALYSIS OF AN ARTICLE

Prior to writing a professional review, the article must be well understood within its parts and as a whole. Thus, I will discuss what one should be looking for in each section of a standard journal article and how it should be cohesive. Standard empirical article sections include, in order: an abstract, introduction, theory, methods, results and conclusions. Other types of articles that may be qualitative and pure theory will have slightly different expected contents and formats, but many of the principles discussed for the empirical article apply. A theory article will not have methods and results sections and the theory section will be much more thorough, not only including existing theory, but also developing additional new theory more than would be found in an empirical article that would either test existing theory or extend theory, but not as expansively. The purpose of a qualitative article may be, for example, to develop theory by using a grounded approach; the theory may actually develop out of the methods and results, a different order (Singleton and Straits, 1988). Any related existing theory would be discussed in advance.

The abstract is often ignored in PhD seminars, but reviewers consider it critical in forming their impression as to whether they will have a positive reaction to the article or not. It may be a case of first impressions, but if the abstract does not do what's expected, a reviewer will wonder how much worse the article is going to be given that an abstract is relatively easy to write. Also, clarity in the abstract is an initial indication of the quality and clarity of thought in the paper. The abstract should be written last, after the paper is finished and tells the reader what the paper intends to do, how it does it and what the results are within a limited word length, usually 100–300 words. An author may use catchphrases to grab the reader's attention so that he or she will read on.

The introduction section can be written using different approaches, but has some main ingredients. A choice of style can be made in the beginning. For example, it may start by introducing the theoretical stream of the paper to emphasize its intention to engage in theory building. It may begin with an interesting anecdote to capture the imagination of the reader, put the paper into a context of general or recent interest, or provide a real world analogy so that when the paper becomes abstract, the reader can keep a familiar analogy in mind. Another possibility is to begin with a recent issue or event of importance, like the financial crisis, and link the question of the paper to this important issue or event. The paper could also begin by discussing the context in which it intends to test hypotheses. Particular industry or international issues could be a way to introduce the testing context when it is an important element of the paper. However, sometimes the intent to test theory is so much the focus that the empirical context is irrelevant except as it makes the theory more or less generalizable or influences data accessibility or limitations. In a case like this, the context should not be discussed so early because it gives it too much emphasis. Most importantly, this part of the introduction should somehow grab the interest of the academic group to which it is aimed.

An important element of the introduction is the research question with some explanation of why it's being investigated and why it is important to do so. It's usually investigated because there is a theoretical gap in the literature that has some value in addressing for theory building. Another reason to ask a particular question in an empirical paper is because although the theory has been written, it needs testing and if it's been tested, perhaps there is a better methodological approach or it needs to be tested in a more or another generalizable setting. The introduction does not include a thorough explanation of the theoretical gap because that often entails an in-depth review of past research. In some research streams, phenomena are investigated rather than testing theory. This happens frequently in the international business literature, for example, and it is criticized for having this emphasis.

Additionally, the introduction usually indicates the level or units of analysis of the study such as the individual, firm or organization, industry or population, and community levels, where a community is a set of populations (Carroll, 1984). Sometimes, papers study at more than one level of analysis, but the main issue is to keep attributions consistent. An ecological fallacy occurs when the levels or units of analysis are mixed such that the relationships between properties of groups or geographical areas are used to make inferences about the individual behaviors of the people within those groups or areas (Singleton and Straits, 1988).

The theory section may not be titled as such, but it should have a descriptive title to suggest that some background theory will be discussed. Several sections may be required in case the paper draws from several theoretical traditions. It is in this section that past work is reviewed, mentioning its important contributions, showing how different papers differ in

4 Research companion to green international management studies

their views, approaches and results. Most importantly, this section should emphasize how the previous literature relates to the current research question and where there is a gap in the current work that is useful to address. It is in this section that the detailed explanation, introduced in the first section, is fleshed out. The theory section is usually written in a matter-of-fact tone; although it is a critique of what has been done, it's usually not an emotional or purposely biased argument.

Next, the author extends theory and either includes propositions if it is a theory paper or hypotheses if it is an empirical paper. The propositions are detailed falsifiable statements that in combination serve to answer the research question (Popper, 1963). If it is an empirical paper this part may simply entail explanations of how the author is arriving at detailed testable and operationalizable hypotheses. However, an empirical paper may also extend theory and the explanations leading to the hypotheses would include this. After each explanation, a proposition or hypothesis should be written. A hypothesis is a more specific version of a falsifiable proposition. An empirical paper uses data that enables the construction of variables; hypotheses will describe the exact relationships, whether correlational or causational, between variables of interest or interactions among them and a dependent variable that is an outcome variable.

If it is an empirical paper it continues with a methods section. Now that the reader is thoroughly convinced of the value of addressing the research question and understands the logic behind testing the hypotheses, what they are and how they link to the research question, there is this technical section that describes the details of the testing. The methods section first describes the data and variables; however, sometimes these are distinct sections prior to the methods section – they may be separated. A description of the data includes names of the data sources, what fields of important information are in the sources, whether there is missing data and how it is dealt with and how the data is coded. For example, an answer to a question may be binary coded yes = 1 and no = 0. The variables are constructed from the data and will usually be given short descriptive names that are also indicative of how they are coded. For example, rather than calling a binary variable that indicates gender, 'gender', it would be called 'female' if female = 1 and male = 0. Sometimes, variables are created through complicated mathematical operations and this should be described in detail. Why is this important? Measurement problems exist when variables, as constructed, do not measure what they are described to measure, the constructs, as laid out in the earlier theory and hypotheses section. Reviewers are careful to examine this issue. Also, a variable that proxies for a construct may not be one in the sense that it does not represent it well or it has limitations or differences. However, the proxy may be the only possible choice and this needs to be explained so that the results can be interpreted with understanding of these limitations. Other problems may arise and this is only a sample discussion. A research methods seminar is suggested for more detail.[1]

The methods are the statistical approach(es) that are used to make the logical connection amongst the variables as laid out in the hypotheses. Very often, reviewers look for problems here. The wrong statistical model may be chosen or various elements of the model may not be chosen correctly. Problems in the direction of causality may be evident and this is frequently referred to as endogeneity; that is, the direction of causality is not obvious such that it could logically go in the reverse direction of that posited in the hypothesis. Also, problems of omitted variables can lead to misspecification; variables that are highly correlated with each other can lead to serial correlation. Many technical statistical problems can occur and this makes empirical work tricky and an easy target for reviewers' negative comments to the point of dismissing results. Very often, when there are many potential technical difficulties with models, extensive additional analysis that finds the model to be sound can satisfy reviewers' inquiries. Refer to statistical texts for the details of these issues (Belsley et al., 1980; Greene, 1993; Wooldridge, 2009).

The results section describes the output of the model(s) that is (are) tested in the methods section. It is important that the results are reported accurately and displayed in a clear manner, usually in tables of results that are discussed. A reviewer cannot likely check whether the results have been reported faithfully; that can only happen if the data is made available so that results can be replicated using the methods approach described in the paper. The way the results are discussed and interpreted should be carefully noted and compared with the original hypotheses. Check whether the author takes an optimistic view as to whether a hypothesis has not been falsified based on pre-specified significance criteria.

A section of conclusions may also include limitations and future research suggestions. The conclusion must answer the research question and it will also discuss whether and to what extent it has made the intended contribution and this could include solving the problem of the research gap, if one was identified. If the paper extends theory then it should explain how it has done so; it is desirable to describe what more can be done in this regard as suggestions for future research. Also, the study approach may have limitations. For example, the data describes a context that is unique or unlike other contexts in which the theory could operate. This means that more testing should be done to check how widely applicable or generalizable is the theory. All identifiable limitations should be explained and, if possible, suggestions for how future research could solve them should be discussed. Depending on the intended audience, policy implications and lessons for managers are mentioned. The implications of the findings and how they may be useful to or impactful on others can be desirable additional comments.

A reviewer does not usually focus a critique on conclusions unless they are very misleading or much more needs to be said that is obviously missing. The substance that a reviewer pays most attention to is found in the theory explaining the propositions or hypotheses, methods and results. Overall, the work in the paper should answer the research question(s) and make a contribution to research that is interesting or valuable. Some like there to be a 'wow' factor in the sense that results or the news of the paper should be surprising; this is desirable, but certainly not necessary in order to make an intellectual contribution.

USING AN OUTLINE

An outline can be a first useful step in developing a review. So that certain elements of a critique are not forgotten, an outline can be filled in based on an understanding of the article. It can help to pinpoint the strengths and weaknesses of an article while also providing a basic summary. With this start, one may begin to think about extending the discussion about the article based on original ideas or other related literature. A blank outline may look like that shown in Figure 1.1.

Using a short form approach to completing the outline above in a couple of pages can help one think beyond the contents of the article or think in more holistic way; after completion, it's been simplified down to the major issues identified and ideas have not been lost because they are recorded in a clear way. As one reads a complicated article, numerous ideas may come to mind and as one issue is thought of, another one pops up and may distract away from the first. Making a record of these things on an outline can avoid this problem. A clear view of the article can also help prioritize the issues; some issues more seriously threaten the integrity of the results and need more work and attention than others. Also, an issue that initially seems problematic may turn out not to be so after it's been given further thought. A reviewer can make follow-up notes on this outline after turning to other sources and as he or she goes through this thought and investigative process.

A first cut at a written review may be the output of this step. It serves as the core critique that includes a brief summary including many of the items in the outline and a discussion of the major strengths and weaknesses. The reviewer has thought about the relative importance of the strengths and

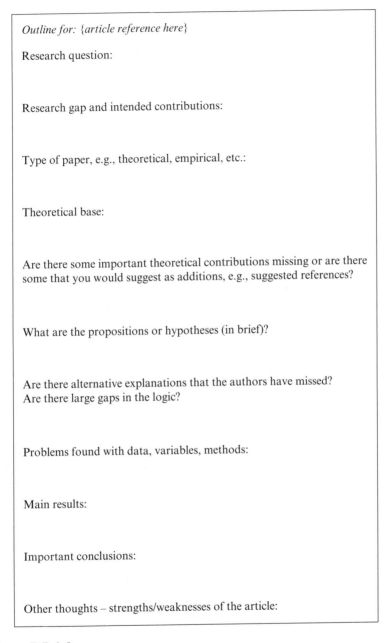

Outline for: {article reference here}

Research question:

Research gap and intended contributions:

Type of paper, e.g., theoretical, empirical, etc.:

Theoretical base:

Are there some important theoretical contributions missing or are there
some that you would suggest as additions, e.g., suggested references?

What are the propositions or hypotheses (in brief)?

Are there alternative explanations that the authors have missed?
Are there large gaps in the logic?

Problems found with data, variables, methods:

Main results:

Important conclusions:

Other thoughts – strengths/weaknesses of the article:

Source: D.E. de Lange

Figure 1.1   An example of a review outline

weaknesses, as suggested above, so as to make as unbiased a decision as possible as to whether the article achieves its intended goal and, in fact, is useful in any way to the field to which it intends to contribute. The review should finish with an overall connected dispassionate opinion.

MAKING IT PROFESSIONAL

A professional review, like a book review, not only conveys the information as mentioned, but is also interesting to read and places emphasis on the most important aspects. It even completely leaves out that which the reviewer chooses not to emphasize for the sake of focusing attention on the important issues. It may include only one major issue and the tone may not be quite so dispassionate as in the first draft, but this must be a careful choice. In designing something that is interesting there very often needs to be some passion and opinion expressed, but only as it seems reasonable, because otherwise the reviewer risks losing credibility in the conveyance of extremism, especially not appropriate in the academic genre. How is a review made interesting aside from using focus? More interesting language, using similes and metaphors, can be one approach if used cautiously. Also, talking about the article in a context of interest to the reviewer or in a manner that makes the article relevant to the world can extend the article beyond its boundaries. For an example, a sustainability article that studies activism could be discussed in reference to the recent Copenhagen climate summit or past WTO protests.

An alternate and possibly most impactful path to take is to discuss the article in the context of its field, but not in such a manner as to repeat the theoretical review that was in the article. Challenging the place the article finds for itself or recognizing a wider impact of the article in its field can provide a fascinating new view. Many additional citations are required such that the critique is not confined to the article of focus. This kind of discussion may not be possible for a couple of reasons, one being that the article has already done this and a second being that the reviewer may not have the knowledge to do this; the field may be too disparate and therefore such a commentary is almost impossible; also, the field may be too large.

I'll make a few final comments. A professional article review must be well-written and conform to a limited word or page length; for a review to be useful, it cannot approach the length of a research article. Its usefulness is in the fact that it conveys the essence of the article, more so than would reading the abstract and conclusions and without having to read the entire article. Moreover, a book review often identifies the audiences that may take an interest in the book and while this is likely less necessary or appropriate in an article review, it may find a place in cases where policy-makers and managers, for example, find the results interesting. More often, it can be assumed that the article is of primary interest to an academic audience simply because it is an academic journal article, thus this doesn't need to be stated in the review. Also, the review should demonstrate a command of the material so as to instill confidence in the reader. If the reader feels that the writer is not reliable or capable, then the review is useless and the reader will feel it necessary to go back and read the article.

NOTE

1. To learn more about research design, refer to the book *Approaches to Social Research* (Singleton and Straits, 1998), listed in the references section. This book contains many of the research principles about which a reviewer should be able to comment.

REFERENCES

Belsley, D.A., Kuh, E. and Welsch, R.E. 1980. *Regression Diagnostics: Identifying Influential Data and Sources of Collinearity*. New Jersey: John Wiley and Sons, Inc.

Carroll, G.R. 1984. Organizational ecology. *Annual Review of Sociology*, **10**: 71–93.

Greene, W.H. 1993. *Econometric Analysis*. New Jersey: Prentice-Hall, Inc.

Popper, K.R. 1963. Science, conjectures and refutations. In K.R. Popper, *Conjectures and Refutations*. London: Routledge and Kegan Paul.

Singleton, Jr, R.A. and Straits, B.C. 1988. *Approaches to Social Research*. Oxford: Oxford University Press.

Wooldridge, J.M. 2009. *Introductory Econometrics: A Modern Approach*. Kentucky: South Western Educational Publishing.

2 An overview of the green international management literature
Deborah E. de Lange

The four areas of reviews in this book: (1) CSR; (2) NGOs, IGOs, Government and Sustainability in Developing Nations; (3) Environmental Innovation and Talent; and (4) Academic Theory were chosen out of an initial larger list of areas proposed to contributors, so these were of particular interest to them. However, the area of green international management and of sustainability, in general, is extremely hard to define in terms of its boundaries or areas that it covers. I have found no conceptual map or taxonomy for this growing literature. It is disorganized.

Consequently, the aim of this section is to review the literature in an organized and analytical way to develop a view of the area. I review it from a very high and general perspective. Also, I will place the work of this book – the journal articles from the review sections – into this wider picture so that we understand how this book fits into the current literature. I will not provide a history of the field because it has been done in articles (Wood, 1991; Starik and Marcus, 2000; Etzion, 2007; Lee, 2008), rather, I am going to focus on what the field looks like now in an attempt to provide a mental map so that researchers may talk about it in a clearer way and also understand how they are developing it. I am going to start by producing a logical framework for categorization, categorize a large body of the literature and see where the 'chips fall', as we say. Certain intersections of categorization will likely contain the bulk of the literature and obvious gaps will arise so this will be telling.

Ultimately, what the concept of sustainability does is expand our view of what is important for human progress. In recent times, economics has had center stage and that has led to a money-oriented business-first agenda in which the primary organizing principle of our actions and organizations is economic and all those other costs that we have such a problem accounting for are 'externalities'. It also places primary importance on those who have the most to gain economically and least importance on others who may experience the externalities. Thus, shareholders in the economic paradigm are in the forefront and all the others, whether individuals or organizations, who we may refer to as additional stakeholders – employees, community members, minority groups, labor unions, non-governmental organizations, and so on – are secondary and rarely matter except as those who conveniently and most often silently shoulder the costs on behalf of shareholders.

Since little effort or emphasis has been placed on understanding how to value these costs and build an accepted system to account for them, they have been dismissed because they are difficult to value and account for. These 'non-quantifiable' costs are conveniently ignored. These costs are further de-emphasized by a culture that values mathematics to such an extent that if it's difficult to quantify, it's not a hard issue, it's a soft issue and such categorization assigns the issue to a low status and priority.

Speaking to scholars studying in this field, I've encountered some opposition to scientific quantitative research approaches. My analysis is that it's not really an opposition to the use of logic or mathematical style theory; it's an opposition to what our approach to logic has left out of its calculations, thus not really being so logical. Our current day approaches to what we call science are narrow and selective of what is conveniently quantifiable. Too many simplifying assumptions must be made to the point that they assume away most of the complexity of the world and that includes people; for example, transaction cost economics' assumptions that people are uniformly selfish and opportunistic (Williamson, 1985).

The concept of sustainability incorporates more complexity and broadens our priorities and actions such that the externalities are internalized. The Brundtland Commission's report, *Our Common Future* Chapter 2, described sustainable development as, 'development that meets the needs of the present without compromising the ability of future generations to meet their own needs'. Elkington (1999) developed the concept of the 'triple bottom line', which proposed that business goals were inseparable from the societies and environments within which they operate. Thus, the three pillars to consider are environmental, social and economic in the context of a long-term view. Once again, this stands in opposition to the primary stakeholders of the economic view, the shareholders, because they motivate our business-oriented organizations towards short-term growth – shareholders want to invest to make gains as soon as possible and this becomes the narrow priority.

Sustainability is very much about how we, humans, choose to live and impact our environment; it's not a philosophy for the natural world. Thus, I'm going to begin the categorization design by using dimensions that encompass our human world together with the three pillars of sustainability. The 'PEST' analysis includes the dimensions: Political, Economic, Social and Technological. Another framework uses the dimensions: Economic, Business, Social, Political and Physical (Gopinath, 2008). The Physical dimension is also meant to incorporate both the technological and natural aspects of the world. I am going to change the 'Physical' dimension to the 'Environmental' dimension in alignment with the three pillar view and keep the Technological category. Also, the Business aspect will merge with the Economic. Thus, I will include the following categorical dimensions: Social, Political, Environmental, Technological and Economic. The Technological dimension could be subsumed under the Environmental because the technologies in the literature will be those that contribute to utilizing alternative resources more efficiently and in cleaner ways.

Additionally, I am going to borrow from Etzion's (2007) work that reviews the organizations and natural environment (ONE) literature by dividing it by levels of analysis. He uses three levels: the individual firm, industry and the firm within its organizational environment. I will generalize such that a firm is an organization, an industry is a collectivity of similar organizations so they are a population and the firm in its organizational environment is an organization in its organizational field – the field contains all entities related to the organization, not only similar types of organizations (Hoffman, 1999; Greenwood et al., 2002; Davis and Marquis, 2005). Rather than including an individual level, he has classified collectivities of individuals, such as consumers and investors, as being at the highest level of the organizational environment since they are stakeholders. I will not include an individual level either since most of the work considered in this text stems from strategy and organizational theory (meso and macro levels) rather than organizational behavior. However, the occasional article may be at the individual level and I will put it in the organizational level because I don't want to include an entire category for these extraneous additions. Most of these will be leadership articles and leaders are attached to their organizations anyway. Additionally, this book is concerned with green *international* management. While the industry level may incorporate multinational corporations, other types of organizations are included that may be international or global such as NGOs. Thus, I am going to add a level of analysis that will be called the international level. When MNCs of an industry are the focus, I will place them into this level of analysis category rather than the industry category since 'industry' could be domestic or international and does not recognize the special international characteristics of a multinational entity.

When classifying articles by level of analysis, I will choose the highest applicable level of analysis. Some articles examine several levels. Also, some articles that may have a particular unit of analysis such as the firm but seem to go beyond this by, for example, examining the field in a looser way, may be classified elsewhere for the sake of recognizing a breadth of analysis that makes it unique. Lumping everything into the firm level does not recognize the differences amongst the articles. This is why the column heading in Table 2.1 is called 'Level or Breadth of Analysis'.

Additionally, a theoretical classification is shown in the table. The dominant theories in sustainability have been the resource-based view (RBV), institutional theory and stakeholder theory. Other theories are used and sometimes no particular theory is used. Sometimes articles use many theories and this may result in a small classification dilemma. For example, if an article uses both RBV and institutional theory, the theory that seems to have the most success in the empirical findings or has more emphasis in the article is chosen as a basis for classification.

No theory specifically for the area of sustainability exists, but stakeholder theory is the closest to this. The connection of the area of study to stakeholder theory is that sustainability considers a wider set of domains than just the economic: economic, social and environmental and, correspondingly, stakeholder theory encompasses a wider set of actors than only shareholders; these actors may represent many of the social and environmental concerns that are additional to the economic mainstay. For example, labor unions are stakeholders who may argue for health and safety concerns on behalf of employees and these would be social issues. Additionally, the resource-based view has been adjusted to become the natural-resource-based view (Hart, 1995); this existing theory has been specialized and perhaps is an improvement on the original theory.

Table 2.1 contains a large body of the literature on sustainability that has been classified as aforementioned. The reviewed articles that are included in this book have an asterisk to identify them. The other articles are considered by scholars and experts in the field as important as, for example, they are included in PhD course syllabi. The list also serves as an excellent source from which to choose literature for designing a PhD seminar in sustainability.

RESEARCH CONTRIBUTION EMPHASES AND DEFICIENCIES

The following discussion examines the distribution of articles in Table 2.1 along various lines so as to see where the research has been concentrated and where it may gravitate toward in order to address deficiencies. Some figures have been created to support this analysis, as follows. As expected, the social (26 percent) and environmental (58 percent) domains take precedence in the sustainability literature (see Figure 2.1), according to the count of all articles in Table 2.1. Few articles fall into the political, technological and economic classifications, 16 percent in total, and most

Table 2.1 Classification table for sustainability literature

Dimension	Level or Breadth of Analysis	Paper & Dominant Theory				
		Resource-based view	Institutional theory	Stakeholder theory	Other	None
Social	Organization/Firm	Bowen (2007) Marcus & Anderson (2006)	Campbell (2007) Terlaak (2007)	Hillman & Keim (2001)* Margolis & Walsh (2003)* Clarkson (1995) Garriga & Mele (2004) Orlitsky et al. (2003)	Lewis (2000)* Roberts (2003)* Carroll (1979) McWilliams & Siegel (2001) Scherer & Palazzo (2007) Swanson (1999)	Banerjee (2008)* Hull & Rothenberg (2008)* Lewis (2003)* Lynes & Andrachuk (2008)* Rose (2007)* Abbott & Monsen (1979) Austin et al. (2006) Bies et al. (2007) Mattingly & Berman (2006) McWilliams & Siegel (2000)

Level of analysis				
Population/Industry Organizational Field/ Organizational Environment	Wry (2009)	Harrison & Freeman (1999)	Den Hond & De Bakker (2007) Mair & Marti (2006) Wartick & Cochran (1985) Wood (1991)	Szekely & Knirsch (2005)*
International	Husted & Allen (2006)* Matten & Moon (2008)	Aguilera et al. (2007)		Matten & Crane (2005)*
Political Organization/ Firm Population/ Industry Organizational Field/ Organizational Environment		Sharma & Henriques (2005)*		
International		Teegan et al., Vachani (2004)*	Parker & Pearson (2005)* Rudra (2002)*	Weidenbaum (2009)*

Table 2.1 (continued)

Dimension	Level or Breadth of Analysis	Paper & Dominant Theory				
		Resource-based view	Institutional theory	Stakeholder theory	Other	None
Environmental	Organization/ Firm	Hart (1995)* Christmann (2000) Darnall & Edwards (2006) Judge & Douglas (1998) Russo & Fouts (1997)	Bansal & Clelland (2004)* Berrone & Gomez-Mejia (2009)* Bansal (2005) Delmas & Toffel (2004)	Eesley & Lenox (2006)* King (2007)* Tello & Yoon (2008)* Ambec & Lanoie (2008) Buysse & Verbeke (2003) Chatterji et al. (2008) Kassinis & Vafeas (2006)	Dowell et al. (2000)* Jaffe et al. (2005)* Bowen (2002) Branzei et al. (2004) Cordano & Frieze (2000) Darnell (2005) Dean & McMullen (2007) Hilliard (2004) Jiang & Bansal (2003) Kassinis & Vafeas (2002) King & Lenox (2002)	Andersson & Bateman (2000)* Boiral et al. (2008)* Chen (2008)* Egri & Herman (2000)* Ilinitch & Schaltegger (1995)* Anton et al. (2004) Bansal & Hunter (2003) Bansal (2003) Dyllick & Hockerts (2002) Gerde & Logsdon (2001) Hart & Ahuja (1996)

Population/Industry	Sharma & Vredenburg (1998)* Marcus & Geffen (1998)	King & Lenox (2000)		Russo & Harrison (2005) Sharma (2000) Sharma & Nguan (1999) Siegel (2009) Sharma et al. (1999)	Henriques & Sadorsky (1999) Khanna & Anton (2002) Konar & Cohen (1997, 2001) Majumdar & Marcus (2001) Shrivastava (1995) Toffel & Marshall (2004)
Organizational Field/ Organizational Environment	Aragon-Correa & Sharma (2003)	Jennings & Zandbergen (1995)* Maguire & Hardy (2009)* Delmas & Toffel (2008) Hoffman (1999)	DesJardins (1998) Starik & Marcus (2000)	Hoffman & Ocasio (2001)* Starkey & Crane (2003)* Starik & Rands (1995)* Bansal & Roth (2000) Cohen & Winn (2007)	Berkhout & Rowlands (2007) Chertow (2000) Dunlap & Van Liere (2008) Hamilton (1995) Potoski & Prakash (2005)

Table 2.1 (continued)

Dimension	Level or Breadth of Analysis	Paper & Dominant Theory				
		Resource-based view	Institutional theory	Stakeholder theory	Other	None
	International	Rugman & Verbeke (1998)* Kolk & Pinske (2008)* Nehrt (1998)	Maguire & Hardy (2006)*	Christmann (2004)*	Delmas & Keller (2005) Gladwin et al. (1995) King et al. (2005) Tenbrunsel et al. (2000)	Rowlands (2001)*
Technological	Organization/ Firm			Wagner (2007)*	Gonzalez (2009) Horbach (2008)* Larson (2000)*	Del Rio (2009)* Thompson & Khare (2008)*
	Population/ Industry					

Level of analysis		
Organizational Field/		
Organizational Environment		
International	Reinstaller (2005)*	Giovannucci & Ponte (2005)*, Van Alphen et al. (2009)*
Economic — Organization/Firm	Wiklund & Shepherd (2003)*	Agle et al. (2008)*, Laszlo et al. (2005)*, Agle et al. (1999)
Population/Industry		
Organizational Field/		
Organizational Environment		
International	Oetzel & Doh (2009)*	Sreekumar & Parayil (2002)*, Douglas & Judge (2001)

Note: *A paper that is reviewed in this book. All other papers are part of the larger body of sustainability literature.

Source: Author's own compilation.

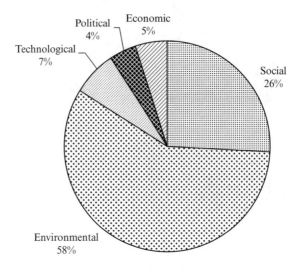

Source: The author.

Figure 2.1   *Articles by domain proportion*

of them were part of the set of journal articles reviewed in this book shown more specifically in Figure 2.5. Thus, the approach of choosing interesting subfields of sustainability prior to searching for articles pressed reviewers to seek out articles related to these specific subtopics that may not otherwise be what is considered part of the main body, or 'mainstream', of the literature. For example, the Environmental Innovation and Talent group chose many of the Technological domain articles.

Also, see Figures 2.2 and 2.3 to examine the distribution of the use of theory in the articles. Overall, most articles do use some theory (68 percent) and more than a third uses one of the main theories (36 percent): resource-based view (10 percent), institutional theory (11 percent) and stakeholder theory (15 percent).[1] Stakeholder theory is relatively popular. Noticing that still 31 percent of the articles use no theory, there is likely a great deal of phenomena-driven and practice-oriented work. It will also be interesting to drill down further to see whether there is another emerging dominant theory in the 'Other' category, to be discussed later. Out of the main theories, the social domain uses stakeholder theory most often whereas the environmental domain uses them more equally, using RBV more than the social domain. This seems to match the theories with the domains since stakeholder theory recognizes social aspects to a more fine-grained level by dividing up the types of actors, whereas RBV, being about 'resources', can acknowledge physical or natural resources more

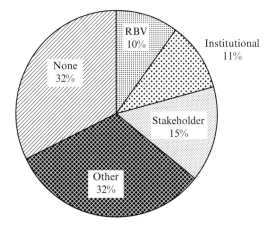

Source: The author.

Figure 2.2   Distribution of theory across all articles

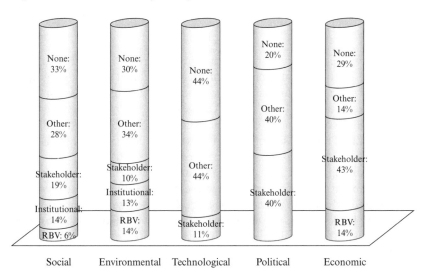

Source: The author.

Figure 2.3   Theory distribution by domain for all articles

prominently (natural-resource-based view). The technological domain uses more 'Other' theories, perhaps being influenced by economics. The political domain uses stakeholder theory and this matches the domain since political discourse is concerned with identifying powerful actors;

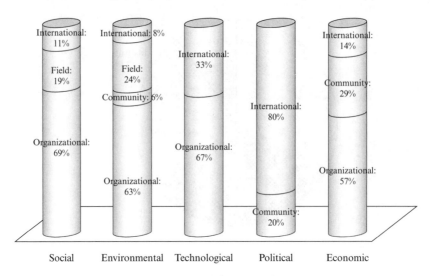

Figure 2.4   Distribution of use of levels of analysis by domain for all articles

however, when one thinks of the institutions that result from this domain, it is surprising that institutional theory is not used and this is a suggestion for future research. Surprisingly, the economic set of articles has used stakeholder theory and the 'Other' category is not large; the 'Other' category would have included economic theories; this odd distribution may be the result of a small sample size of these types of articles, which is to be expected since there was no purposeful economic subfield.

In examining Figure 2.4, the organizational (or firm) level of analysis is predominant in all domains except the political domain and this is to be expected. Most data exists at this level. Clearly, research opportunities exist at higher levels of analysis than the organization. However, the political domain normally talks at the nation state or international level and the subfield was specifically oriented to this level of analysis.

I consider what I will refer to as 'the mainstream literature' to be characterized by the pattern of articles not reviewed in this book since these additional articles were chosen from expert-recommended lists that may be used as PhD syllabi. Scholars choose selectively important and seminal articles for PhD seminars. Some overlap between the lists and reviewed articles exist, but not significantly. Thus, I can compare the pattern of distribution of the types of articles chosen for this book and the pattern of the mainstream articles to see roughly how representative the selection in this book is of the mainstream literature.

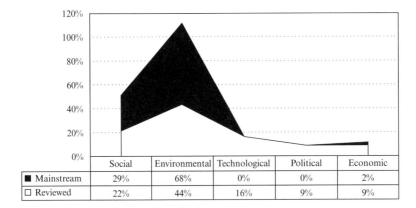

	Social	Environmental	Technological	Political	Economic
■ Mainstream	29%	68%	0%	0%	2%
□ Reviewed	22%	44%	16%	9%	9%

Source: The author.

Figure 2.5 Separate, stacked distributions of reviewed and mainstream article sets, by domain

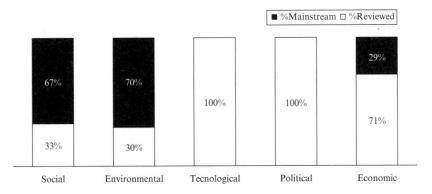

Source: The author.

Figure 2.6 Proportions of reviewed and mainstream articles in the entire set

Taking a look at Figure 2.5, which shows the distribution of the 'mainstream' articles and that of this book, a comparison shows that they are similar in the sense that social and environmental articles are dominant, with environmental articles being the majority. Since the workshop asked participants to look for other types of articles, according to the subgroup they were in, then the 'reviewed' set is broader. Particularly in the political and technological domains, this represents research opportunities. These areas that have one or only a few articles

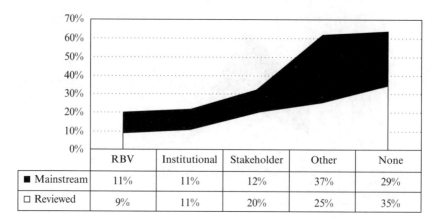

	RBV	Institutional	Stakeholder	Other	None
■ Mainstream	11%	11%	12%	37%	29%
□ Reviewed	9%	11%	20%	25%	35%

Source: The author.

Figure 2.7   Theoretical distribution in the two article sets

provide a base from which to start without having completed a thorough examination.

Looking at the article set as a whole, see Figure 2.6, all the technological and political articles come from the reviewed set, 71 percent of the economic articles were in the reviewed set, 70 percent of the environmental articles were in the mainstream set and 67 percent of the social articles were in the mainstream set.

In examining the theoretical distribution in the two article sets, see Figure 2.7, Stakeholder theory has a bit more weight in the reviewed (20 percent) than in the mainstream set (12 percent), but overall, the percentages for the main theories in the two sets are fairly similar, only differing by percentages in the single digits. The reviewed and mainstream sets seem to be switched in their weightings of 'Other' theory versus no theory. The reviewed set has 'Other' theory in the twentieth percentile (25 percent) whereas the mainstream set is in the thirtieth (37 percent) percentile and vice versa for the 'None' category (35 percent versus 29 percent, respectively). Thus, the mainstream slightly weights theory more compared with no theory than do the reviewers in this book. This was not expected since the workshop included an entire subgroup devoted to examining academic theory in sustainability research. Even so, the reviewed articles are weighted to almost two-thirds in favor of theory versus no theory.

Figure 2.8 shows an appropriate result in the distributions of levels of analysis. The intention in the workshop was to emphasize the international level of analysis and the reviewed articles are more heavily weighted at the

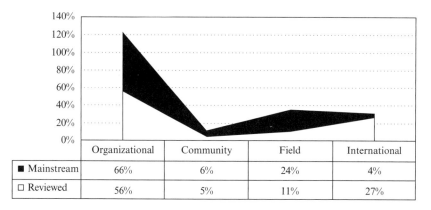

	Organizational	Community	Field	International
■ Mainstream	66%	6%	24%	4%
☐ Reviewed	56%	5%	11%	27%

Source: The author.

Figure 2.8   Distribution of levels of analysis in the two article sets

international level than is the mainstream (27 percent versus 4 percent). It appears that the field level contains some of the difference, being higher in the mainstream set. Otherwise, the organizational and population level weightings are relatively similar, as expected, each lower in the reviewed set than in the mainstream set because of the international emphasis in the reviewed set.

Based on these statistics, the set of articles reviewed in this book seems to capture the pattern of the mainstream closely enough to consider the book quite a good representation with more breadth. Also, it is slightly less theoretical and more international than the main body of the literature.

THEORETICAL USE AND DEVELOPMENT IN THE DOMINANT DOMAINS

As found in the prior section, the dominant domains of this literature are the environmental and social realms. I will examine theoretical use and development in these areas. While focusing on the main theories: resource-based view, institutional theory and stakeholder theory, I will also delve deeper to learn what other theories are making progress; perhaps, others are emerging as prominent. Brief reviews of the three main theories are offered first.

Reviews of the Three Main Theories

Resource-based view
The well-known theory, called the resource-based view (RBV) in the strat-egy and organizations literature, was first credited to Edith Penrose (1959) and was rediscovered and popularized by Jay Barney (1991) and other scholars (Wernerfelt, 1984; Peteraf, 1993). The basic theory, RBV, has been modernized into a new version referred to as 'dynamic capabilities' (Teece et al., 1997) or similarly, 'the knowledge-based view of the firm' (Kogut and Zander, 1992; Foss, 1996). I will give basic explanations of the original theory and the new version.

Penrose (1959) asked about the flows of resources for growth of the firm in an effort to develop a general theory of firm growth. She conceptualized the firm as a collection of resources that produce services at the behest of administrators; she called this the creation of the 'productive oppor-tunity' of the firm. Factors that limit the growth of the firm include: (1) internal conditions as a result of managerial limitations on their abilities, (2) conditions outside the firm that include product and factor markets, and (3) internal attitudes and external conditions that are referred to as uncertainty and risk. Some key themes of her view are: (1) that discrete amounts of resources make bundles of possible services, (2) uncertainty and risk in both internal and external conditions, as mentioned, and (3) diversification. Firm growth could arise by using the services to make final products or to expand and diversify the firm. So, she focused on some very concrete concepts around tangible resources and, in a way, matter (resources) changing to energy (services) while integrating some psychological human factors such as uncertainty and perceptions of risk. However, the human factors are limiting more than growth enhancing. Production is growth whereas the psychological factors, control of admin-istrators, and managers are limitations.

Barney (1991) also focuses on resources, but recognizes three sources: physical, human and organizational capital, allowing more emphasis on positive human- and organizational-level contributions to what he terms the firm's sustainable competitive advantage. He wants to draw a link between the firm's heterogeneous resources and sustainable competi-tive advantage; how does the former translate into the latter? A firm's ability to develop a uniqueness using its resources can maintain success in the sense that it generates 'rents' – revenues. The resources should be valuable, rare, imperfectly imitable and organizationally specific (VRIO). Some key concepts behind imperfect imitability include: (1) unique his-torical conditions that lead to acquisition of unique resources, (2) causal ambiguity that makes it hard to understand the linkage of the resources to competitive advantage, and (3) social complexity that may be related to organizational cultural attributes, difficult to socially re-engineer (Barney, 1991; Peteraf, 1993). It is a holistic view that sees the firm as a complex brew of many unique aspects interwoven into a complete form. It is hard for one firm to copy another because it would try to find aspects to copy and incorporate into its own functioning, but it cannot incorporate the aspects it tries to copy because it is too different in many ways. A popular example is in the airline industry and the success of Southwest Airlines compared with, for example, Continental. The latter, larger airline cannot incorporate the successful aspects of the short haul, low cost, low fare, friendly airline into its operations because they are so fundamentally different. Continental may as well run two separate businesses.

The dynamic capabilities view is an evolution of RBV developed primarily because of criticisms that it is tautological; heterogenous resources are competitive advantage and, moreover, competitive advantage is also derived from them. RBV also has limitations in regards to the type of environment it expects. For Teece et al. (1997), dynamic capabilities refers to the firm's capacity to renew competences so as to maintain competitive advantage in a changing business environment; strategic management has an important role in adapting, integrating and reconfiguring internal and external organizational skills, resources and functional competences to match turbulent markets (ibid.). An additional implication is that firms are not viewed as a bundle of contracts necessarily composed of shirking, selfish actors (Williamson, 1975, 1985; Kogut and Zander, 1992; Foss, 1996). Instead, a firm is a repository of distinct productive (technological and organizational) knowledge that must also be a social community so that knowledge can be learned, produced and commercially applied (Kogut and Zander, 1992; Foss, 1996). Eisenhardt and Martin (2000) discuss the dynamic capabilities view as process- rather than resource-oriented in fast-changing environments in which knowledge is key. They are trying to avoid the vague abstractions (e.g., social complexity) and tautology of RBV and explain that processes such as product development, alliancing and strategic decision-making are concrete means that contribute to strategy (ibid.). They also express some disagreement with RBV such that advantageous practices may not be so unique; many firms through equifinality implement similar practices. Also, firms develop adaptive routines, difficult to sustain, that are useful in situations of fast-changing environments. Helfat's (1997) empirical work explains that firms facing change, such as those in the oil industry during the 1970s and 1980s when prices shot up, use a combination of innovative new knowledge and assets to develop alternative strategies. The oil industry discovered cheaper synthetic fuels. The ability to incorporate new R&D was a dynamic capability that allowed them to evolve so as to match rapidly changing market conditions. Helfat and Peteraf (2003) introduce the capability lifecycle (CLC) that includes heterogeneous resources and capabilities. They explain how this heterogeneity arises through three stages somewhat analogous to the product lifecycle, thus turning again to a process approach. It's a generic framework that claims to be able to explain the development of any capability such as alliance formation, for example (ibid.).

Institutional theory
Institutional theory's main thrust is that organizational conformity builds legitimacy so that an organization can obtain the resources it needs for survival (Meyer and Rowan, 1977). Legitimacy is the primary resource (ibid.). Institutionalization is the process by which societal expectations of appropriate form or behavior come to take on a rule-like status in social thought and action (DiMaggio and Powell, 1983). Organizations will attempt to incorporate the rationalized myths and social norms and beliefs of the institutional environment in order to build legitimacy (ibid.). The theory is cognitively based and environmentally deterministic.

The environment of bounded organizations includes the state, professional organizations, society and members of the inter-organizational field (Meyer and Rowan, 1977; DiMaggio and Powell, 1983). It is collective and interconnected. The degree of institutionalization reflects the extent to which norms or beliefs are broadly diffused or widely shared. An organization survives by conforming and adhering to the external criteria of appropriate behavior and structure. Furthermore, it seeks to adopt external legitimated elements to attain legitimacy itself. The resulting isomorphism is a positive force that may be coercive, mimetic or normative (DiMaggio and Powell, 1983). Organizations are effective as a consequence of conformity, persistence and legitimacy and not necessarily because they are efficient (Meyer and Rowan, 1977). Legitimacy is the resource; otherwise, resources play no role in this theory.

Meyer and Rowan (ibid.) explain that the structure of organizations is determined by institutional rules, norms and beliefs. Institutional pressures and expectations affect structure, especially adding to or elaborating structure in response to complexity. Organizations change through reproduction, imitation and adoption of external norms. Inertia is a function of history, habit and preconscious processes so the theory focuses on persistence rather than change. Consequently, managers are constrained by convention and taken-for-granted expectations; their actions are dictated by existing scripts, routines and myths.

Overall, organizations succeed by accommodating not only the market and competitive pressures, but also pressures outside the market that come from the government, professional associations and societal opinion (Meyer and Rowan, 1977; DiMaggio and Powell, 1983). Both innovation and conformance are important so an organization must manage both efficiency and legitimacy.

Stakeholder theory
Stakeholder theory describes how organizations operate and attempts to predict organizational behavior (Brenner and Cochran, 1991). It explains and guides the structure and operation of a firm as it is a 'going concern' (Donaldson and Preston, 1995). The corporation is 'an organizational entity through which numerous and diverse participants accomplish multiple, and not always entirely congruent, purposes' (ibid., p.67). This is conceptually consistent with Scott's view of the organization as an open system in the sense that participants have multiple conflicting goals; the organization does not act cohesively or even necessarily in directions that will facilitate its survival (Scott, 1992). However, a stakeholder theory of the firm is inclusive of actors both inside and outside the firm whereas Scott's conception of an organization is primarily concerned with those contained within it. Thus, stakeholder theory could be considered an extension of Scott's view in the context of the business entity rather than generic organizations. However, whether stakeholder theory could be applied to any type of organization is something for scholars to further consider.

The involved theoreticians recognize three ways that the theory is presented and this creates frequently discussed philosophical tension. However, this tension would exist in other theories if the related theoreticians also decided to think in these terms; thus, the issues are not actually confined to this theory. Stakeholder theory may be descriptive, instrumental and normative, but the theory has a normative core (Donaldson and Preston, 1995). The normative view tells managers how their firm 'should' work and the main premises are (1) that stakeholders have legitimate interests in the corporation and are defined by their interests in the corporation rather than the corporation's interest in them and (2) stakeholders' interests have intrinsic value, but not equally so (ibid.). The descriptive version simply tells us what the corporation is, whereas the instrumental version attempts to make a causal connection between considering all stakeholders and corporate performance in traditional terms such as market values, profits and revenues. Thus, the premise is that if managers take care of all stakeholders, the firm will perform well. Notice that managers are the brokers who attempt to satisfy the stakeholders. Earlier, the instrumental connection was considered difficult to empirically test, but it has been done by defining and measuring more precise constructs (Hillman and Keim, 2001). Donaldson (1999) has produced an argument to show that a normative discussion is actually inclusive of the instrumental and vice versa. A progressive view is that the goals of instrumentality may be broadened to other than those considered 'traditional' since this is highly culturally and legally determined. 'Traditional' goals of growth, revenues and profits are shareholder oriented and American. However, in other places such as Germany, Japan, Great Britain and the European Community, laws and culture presume interdependencies with and responsibilities to several other parties such as employees, customers, creditors and suppliers.

This view works at all levels of analysis and it can and has been combined with any other organizational theory (Donaldson and Preston, 1995; Hillman and Keim, 2001). Thus, the literature's tone is not to compete with other theories, but rather to combine with and improve them. Ultimately, it broadens the other theories by more specifically recognizing the other entities in the firm's environment. What is often referred to vaguely as 'the environment' in other theories and presented as a backdrop, is highly identified and at the forefront in this theory. The identified environment is composed of primary and secondary stakeholders such that primary stakeholders have a more direct relationship with and investment in the firm whereas secondary stakeholders may or may not choose to be involved with the firm (Hillman and Keim, 2001; Etzion, 2007). For example, employees, customers, creditors, suppliers and community members who are affected by the firm's operations in some way (e.g., environmental effluents, noise, etc.) have little choice but to be affected by and involved with the firm. The media, NGOs and potential employees, for example, may influence the firm, be influenced by the firm and actively support primary stakeholders. These influencers or secondary stakeholders have a choice in their involvement. For example, a newspaper, a secondary stakeholder, may decide to report a firm's neglect of cleaning up its environmental pollution. This report would be in support of the community, a primary stakeholder that is negatively affected.

Theoretical Use and Development of the Main Theories

The following discusses some interesting aspects and themes in the literature that uses each of the theories just reviewed to gain an understanding of what the direction of the research has been and where it might be going. This is a more general overview compared with what the Academic Theory group did in its workshop exploration that follows. After in-depth reviews of many articles, it came to consensus about where the theory is directed and where it suggests it may go. While it didn't recommend one theory over another the group did notice that the field has been building on and combining existing theories. The group hinted that challenging current views and theories may be interesting. Within the larger pool of literature, I've confirmed what the group observed, but I've also noticed one trend that may be viewed as a challenge. It is a desire to no longer have to justify this work by satisfying narrow traditional instrumental interests; instead, many scholars would like to break free from this constraining past so as to express the holistic normative truth of this field. However, it is often framed subtly so as to suggest a transition rather than usurpation. Also, at least a few scholars have analyzed two or more theories at a time so as to recommend one over another for sustainability studies. In order, I will discuss the trends in the resource-based view, institutional theoretic and stakeholder theoretic papers and I will start with one that chooses amongst theories.

Bowen (2007) identifies the resource-based view and the behavioral theory of the firm (Cyert and March, 1963) as competing theories applicable to corporate social strategy. Corporate social strategy is 'the firm's plan to allocate resources in order to achieve long-term social objectives and create a competitive advantage' (Husted and Allen, 2000, p.25). She recognizes the problems that neoclassical economics has in its treatment of firm social strategy; social issues are externalities and completely separated from the core business (Bowen, 2007). The assumptions of the other theories improve upon this latter view and are therefore more likely able to deal with social strategy. Her intended contribution is not to create a new theory or encourage scholars to combine the ones she prefers. Instead, she aims to highlight the aspects of each theory that explain social strategy. She slightly prefers the behavioral theory of the firm over the resource-based view because it recognizes competing goals and social complexity (ibid.).

Marcus and Anderson (2006) focus on the dynamic capability view that is associated with RBV. They explore whether a dynamic capability that is a business competence could also be a social competency and find that this is not the case. They decide that what drives competitive advantage (business competencies) does not necessarily drive social responsibility (social competencies do). Thus, different goals have different drivers. Essentially, they are exploring how to apply RBV concepts to corporate social strategy. It is not an attempt to extend the existing theory.

Hart (1995) is a seminal paper that seeks to extend RBV so that it is applicable to the firm in its natural environment. RBV has been an internally focused theory, but competitive advantage comes from internal and external factors. He calls it the natural-resource-based view (NRBV) of the firm. The strategies Hart considers important include pollution prevention, product stewardship and sustainable development. While Marcus and Anderson (2006) accept RBV as it is and conclude that it separates business from social responsibility issues, Hart decides that competitive advantage is derived through the firm's relationship with its natural environment. He changes the theory. Thus, a business competency would be social responsibility because being socially responsible is a source of competitive advantage; it's not a separate goal. This extension is an evolution of the theory not only applicable to the field of sustainability. Without it, firms will miss the environment as an important source for building sustainable competitive advantage (Hart, 1995). NRBV should replace RBV in all strategy and organizations literature.

Aragon-Correa and Sharma (2003) extend Hart's NRBV to be a contingent version such that the general business environment plays an important role in the development and effectiveness of a proactive environmental strategy. The general business environment moderates the competitive value of a proactive corporate environmental strategy in both positive and negative ways depending on environmental characteristics including complexity, uncertainty and munificence.

Christmann (2000) refines, operationalizes and empirically tests Hart's (1995) ideas; she finds that interactions between environmental strategies and a firm's heterogeneous complementary assets lead to cost advantages. Darnall and Edwards (2006) empirically build on this work by adding institutional context complexity in the form of varying ownership structure; they find that the previously proposed RBV influences – complementary assets – and the institutional theory influences affect the costs of adopting environmental strategy. Others also make RBV arguments and empirically test them to find that environmental performance is positively linked to economic returns (Russo and Fouts, 1997; Judge and Douglas, 1998).

This RBV work is primarily instrumental, tying environmental management to economic performance. Only Bowen's work is somewhat normative; she believes that one of RBV's advantages over both the behavioral theory of the firm and neoclassical economics is its potential for providing normative advice (Bowen, 2007, p. 110).

In future research, I wonder if it is possible to expand this natural-resource-based view of the firm that, although it is tied to sustainability, has primarily focused on the natural environment more so than social issues. It could be broadened and called the sustainable-resource-based view (SRBV); scholars could empirically test whether other types of sustainability competencies lead to economic performance.

The use of institutional theory gets a later start than RBV in the sustainability literature. Jennings and Zandbergen (1995) and Hoffman (1999) are some of the early papers and by 2004 it becomes popular. However, institutional theory wasn't revisited within the strategy and organizations field until about 1983 from its roots in 1977 (Meyer and Rowan, 1977; DiMaggio and Powell, 1983). Jennings and Zanbergen (1995) intend to extend institutional theory – they want to change it and direct new research. First, they examine how the concept of ecological sustainability becomes institutionalized and next, they offer an institutional view of it prior to suggesting theoretical modifications. Clearly, the goals of this paper are not instrumental as they were in the RBV literature. These researchers are not trying to solve a problem for the firm, that is, to reassure firms that sustainability is profitable for them or tell them how it can be profitable. Instead, the goal is to explain how firms and organizations can become part of a sustainable world. The researchers are not intending normative instruction; rather, they are using the theory to be descriptive.

However, our current economic system is not actually sustainable; that is, these theories would not be good at describing a sustainable system, because such a system is a goal or normative outcome rather than a reflection of current reality. Therefore, theories that focus on the process by which organizations contribute to sustainability and by which society becomes more sustainable are more useful for describing the current state of the world. Furthermore, theories that make some separation between the process of achieving sustainability versus the content or actual details of what sustainability is deemed to be by society will avoid some of the accusations that we are building prescriptive models (ibid., p. 1023).

Institutional theory is not an adequate description yet because it has not included the wider ecological world. The authors describe the problems of application of institutional theory and offer solutions. The theoretical barriers they describe are many and sound difficult to overcome. They also discuss the process of paradigm change from an institutional theoretic view (Jennings and Zandbergen, 1995).

Hoffman (1999) thinks similarly to Jennings and Zandbergen in the sense that he identifies change as necessary for the institutionalization of environmentalism. Institutional theory focuses on conformity, stability and inertia. Institutional forces are isomorphic, so the theory doesn't seem to be inclusive of change and Hoffman intends to correct this misconception. He proposes that institutional fields form around issues and that field members influence each other to change based on their views. Field-level competition is a force for change. Organizations enter and exit the field and change their power balances. Shocks interrupt the inertia (ibid.).

In this literature there is a trend of combining theories. Bansal (2005) intends to demonstrate the value of integrating institutional theory and the resource-based view through an empirical study that considers how various factors affect corporate sustainable development over time. The institutional factors, mimicry, media pressure and slack are effective in earlier time periods of corporate development whereas international experience, considered a resource-based attribute, is effective at any time. Also, Delmas and Toffel (2004) combine institutional and stakeholder theory to examine the drivers of adoption of environmental management practices; regulation – coercive forces – seems to be the main driver. In this view, stakeholders exert institutional forces. Like previous work discussed, the authors are interested in describing change using institutional theory. Also, they seek to explain the heterogeneity of organizations' strategies in the face of field-level isomorphic pressures.

Few international studies have been done and Matten and Moon (2008) is one of them. It is also very recent work that continues along the strand of differences and change rather than isomorphism and inertia while using institutional theory. It seeks to compare CSR differences in the US and Europe while being applicable to a broader international realm. Also, it discusses the three aspects: descriptive, normative and instrumental issues of CSR in cross-national settings. Maguire and Hardy (2006) and Husted and Allen (2006) are international studies reviewed in this book. The former research is also focused on change using institutional logics and recognizes coercive forces (regulation) and changes in power balances. Like Hoffman (1999), it recognizes discourse around issues as fundamental to institution building and change. The latter research differentiates between local and global CSR.

In this stream of institutional theory applied to sustainability literature, a continuing theme, started by the seminal work of Jennings and Zandbergen (1995), is explaining change by using institutional theory – not often associated with dynamic change because of its dominant language and metaphors – to describe firm- and field-level change toward environmentalism.

Stakeholder theory has been used more than RBV and institutional theory; at the same time, it also seems a likely candidate for combination with other theories. It broadens them by identifying and adding more players and their interests; thus, it also operationalizes the external environment in the case of RBV. Clarkson (1995) is early firm-level research that uses a stakeholder approach to develop and evaluate corporate social performance (CSP) from field-level studies. He advises that it is important to differentiate between social issues and stakeholder concerns where the latter concept helps business people to focus their energies and the former is too ambiguous. Also, his conception of a definition of stakeholders is firm-biased. He chooses stakeholders to be those who are necessary to the firm's survival rather than those who have an interest in the firm. Later firm-level stakeholder theory work by Margolis and Walsh (2003), reviewed in this book, signals a transition in the tone of this literature. It discusses the predominance of the instrumental view over the normative and seeks to find a path to changing the emphasis of earlier work from descriptive and finally, towards a normative view of the firm that better considers the rights of stakeholders vis à vis the firm. Some papers are examples of this trend (Garriga and Mele, 2004; Tello and Yoon, 2008).

Aguilera et al. (2007) take a completely different point of view while at the same time working at all levels of analysis, including the international level. They examine stakeholder motivations for pressuring a firm to adopt CSR rather than thinking about how the firm defines and reacts to stakeholders. Stakeholders have instrumental, relational and moral reasons for engaging with the firm. Christmann (2004), reviewed in this book, also takes this stakeholder pressure view from an international-level perspective on MNCs.

Notice that in each theoretical vein, a seminal paper sets the tone for most future work. In RBV, Hart (1995) connects the natural environment to sustainable competitive advantage and changes the theory. Most papers empirically test and extend his ideas while maintaining instrumentality. The occasional paper challenges this connection of the social with firm goals (Marcus and Anderson, 2006) and this is in alignment with the seminal paper in stakeholder theory that wants to clarify to whom the business should pay attention based on business priorities, not social priorities (Clarkson, 1995). However, stakeholder theorists tend to move in another direction, emphasizing a definition of stakeholders that is focused on their interests rather than those of the firm. Although all theoretic streams discuss the competing descriptive, instrumental and normative views, it is in stakeholder theory that this discussion is most contentious; this area has the strongest movement toward normative discourse. Finally, institutional theorists find in Jennings and Zandbergen (1995) a seminal work that motivates the community to describe change that institutionalizes environmentalism. From the start, these researchers dealt with the philosophical tension and chose to be, less controversially, descriptive. Others seem to have followed.

Theoretical Use and Development – Emerging Patterns?

Next, I will review a sample of the literature that falls into the 'Other' theory category in Table 2.1 to see whether there is any dominant movement or emerging pattern toward the use or building of another theory.

Corporate social performance (CSP) is of interest to several scholars and has a continuing stream of literature. Carroll's (1979) seminal three-dimensional conceptual model of corporate performance is not theoretical; rather it is a normative discourse about what the considerations and bounds of social responsibility are for managers. It provides a framework for managers to think about what the firm should do. One dimension is a list of social issues, for example, occupational safety, a second dimension is the social responsibility categories, for example, legal, ethical, and a third dimension is the philosophy of social responsiveness, for example, does the firm strive to be simply reactive or proactive? Wartick and Cochran (1985) build on the corporate social performance model of Carroll (1979); CSP is not really theory yet, but Wartick and Cochran (1985) offer the most modern framework. It's a set of ideas in search of theory. DesJardins (1998) would like to see a theory of CSP using a view from a more sustainable version of economics than the traditional market-based type. As Wood (1991) explains there is still not a theory of CSP, but there are disparate concepts and models that do not yet allow for research questions to be addressed. She attempts to strengthen the concepts in CSP and build some linkages. Swanson (1999) proposes a research strategy for the area of CSP based on first integrating the descriptive and normative strands as an underpinning for theory building. The paper very nicely compares and contrasts models of CSP (Carroll, 1979; Wartick and Cochran, 1985; Wood, 1991) so as to identify their relative normative content. The future intended theory is unclear because the research question(s) aren't outlined and there were no examples of testable propositions. Scherer and Palazzo (2007) continue the line of research in CSP that is concerned with the philosophical approach. They don't prefer either of the positivist or post-positivist approaches and instead, propose a new one based on Habermas's theory of deliberative democracy. The positivist approach is designed to fit in with an economic theory of the firm. A post-positivist view relies on normative philosophical theory.

Sanjay Sharma and his colleagues do follow a consistent and fruitful line of theoretical research that includes some empirical work. However, not many other researchers are jumping on this bandwagon yet. Sharma and Nguan (1999) are concerned with preservation of biodiversity through the work of biotechnology companies in the north working in poorer southern nations. It is a risk for managers to enter into biodiversity conservation strategies with southern nations because they may be required to share technology and profits due to what they perceive as lax intellectual property laws. Their interpretations that influence organizational decisions are analyzed in the context of the managerial cognition literature (Dutton and Jackson, 1987; Jackson and Dutton, 1988; Thomas and McDaniel, 1990; Sharma et al., 1999) (also called strategic issue interpretation literature). It is a threat–opportunity framework that includes three dimensions: positive–negative impact on job or firm performance, economic gain–loss, and controllable–uncontrollable impacts of the business on the environment. The more that the strategy is viewed as an opportunity on these dimensions than a threat, the more likely is the manager to enter into a related agreement (Sharma and Nguan, 1999). Sharma et al. (1999) build on the managerial cognition literature using the threat–opportunity framework to examine what factors affect managerial interpretations of environmental issues and how these interpretations affect strategies of corporate environmental responsiveness. Sharma (2000) also uses this threat–opportunity framework to examine the motivations for the choice of reactive versus proactive environmental strategies in Canada's oil and gas industry. It also considers the influence of organizational context on managerial interpretations. Cordano and Frieze (2000) use Ajzen's theory of planned behavior in an empirical study to examine the attitudes of managers that lead to environmentally sound behaviors such as the implementation of source reduction activities, which is part of pollution prevention.

A related and potentially promising line of research that has been started using theory but not capitalized upon is one that uses an attention-based view of the firm (Ocasio, 1997). Tenbrunsel et al. (2000) draw from organization behavior, behavioral decision theory and social psychology research on goal setting and motivation to support the notion that a situational feature can direct attention toward itself and lead to the neglect of other features. They use behavioral decision theory and psychology research to examine why this phenomenon occurs. Hoffman and Ocasio (2001) ask what prompts public attention to industry events, for example when there is a chemical spill, and build on existing theories of public attention to address this question.

Entrepreneurialism is a theme in this literature sample, but it's disconnected. Mair and Marti (2006) draw upon embeddedness theory to provide a view of social entrepreneurship as a process that catalyzes social change (Burt, 1992, 1997; Gargiulo and Bernassi, 1999). Dean and McMullen (2007) view entrepreneurialism as a vehicle for solving environmental problems that in economic language are market failures, but are viewed as viable business opportunities if consumers are willing to pay for the solutions. Cohen and Winn (2007), from an economic perspective, identify four market imperfections that have contributed to environmental degradation, explore their role as sources of entrepreneurial opportunity and introduce the concept of sustainable entrepreneurship (Coase, 1937; Williamson, 1985, 1991).

Economists make a disparate contribution that tends to be instrumental. DesJardins (1998) wants to use a model of sustainable economics rather than neoclassical economics to build corporate social responsibility theory. Siegel (2009) takes an instrumental view regarding sustainability practices. The economist's theory of the firm perspective is used to discuss why green management should only be implemented if complementary to the firm's profit goal.

Other phenomena of interest include the concept of an ecologically sustainable organization and the behavior of activists. Starik and Rands (1995) build on the concept of what is an ecologically sustainable organization (ESO). They use a mix of organizational theory such as Scott's (1992) open systems view of organizations and the strategic choice view (Child, 1972). Den Hond and De Bakker (2007) use social movement and institutional change theory to explore how activism influences corporate social change activities. Activists aim to bring about field-level change and use different influence tactics because of their varying ideologies.

In reviewing this literature that uses 'Other' theories in Table 2.1, there does not seem to be any emerging pattern of theory use or theory building. The most dominant theoretical line uses cognitive explanations like the managerial cognition and attention-based views. Also, there is a relatively large stream of CSP literature that is struggling to move out of the framework or model phase towards solid theory building that can address research questions.

CONCLUSION

With so much of the sustainability literature not focused on theory building we can see there are opportunities for strengthening this field. Each theoretical area including RBV, institutional theory and stakeholder theory has had its roots in a seminal article that others have built upon, but each has been a relatively narrow path, sometimes with minor changes. Other researchers have attempted to start new theoretical streams that are cognitive or attention-based, but they don't seem to have attracted many others to join them, except perhaps as co-authors. Many ideas are written as conceptual models and frameworks, but have not progressed to the point of becoming sophisticated theoretical output.

Researchers may think to turn to these pages when they make decisions about their next article so that they are building a field and contributing to some logical progression rather than continuing the haphazardness. A multi-theoretic approach is interesting and diversity should be encouraged, but some continuity in each of these streams, even if it is to challenge and change direction, would make the field more substantial and better understood by the audiences these academics intend to influence.

NOTE

1. Remember that this is only roughly accurate. If an article used one of the main theories then it was counted this way, but it could have also used an additional theory, whether one of the other main theories or an 'Other' theory.

REFERENCES

Abbott, W. and Monsen, R.J. 1979. On the measurement of corporate social responsibility: Self-reported disclosures as a method of measuring corporate social involvement. *Academy of Management Journal*, **22**(3): 501–15.

Agle, B.R., Mitchell, R.K. and Sonnenfeld, J.A. 1999. Who matters to CEOs? An investigation of stakeholder attributes and salience, corporate performance, and CEO values. *Academy of Management Journal*, **42**(5): 507–25.

Agle, B.R., Donaldson, T., Freeman, R.E., Jensen, M.C., Mitchell, R.K. and Wood, D.J. 2008. Dialogue: Toward superior stakeholder theory. *Business Ethics Quarterly*, **18**(2): 153–90.

Aguilera, R.V., Rupp, D.E., Williams, C.A. and Ganapathi, J. 2007. Putting the S back in corporate social responsibility: A multilevel theory of social change in organizations. *Academy of Management Review*, **32**(3): 836–63.

Ambec, S. and Lanoie, P. 2008. Does it pay to be green? A systematic overview. *Academy of Management Perspectives*, **22**(4): 45–62.

Andersson, L. and Bateman, T. 2000. Individual environmental initiative: Championing natural environmental issues in U.S. business organizations. *Academy of Management Journal*, **43**(4): 548–70.

Anton, W.R.Q., Deltas, G. and Khanna, M. 2004. Incentives for environmental self-regulation and implications for environmental performance. *Journal of Environmental Economics and Management*, **48**(1): 632–54.

Aragon-Correa, J.A. and Sharma, S. 2003. A contingent resource-based view of proactive corporate environmental strategy. *Academy of Management Review*, **28**(1): 71–88.

Austin, J., Stevenson, H. and Wei-Skillern, J. 2006. Social and commercial entrepreneurship: Same, different, or both? *Entrepreneurship Theory & Practice*, **30**(1): 1–22.

Banerjee, S.B. 2008. Corporate social responsibility: The good, the bad and the ugly. *Critical Sociology*, **34**(1): 51–79.

Bansal, P. 2003. From issues to actions: The importance of individual concerns and organizational values in responding to natural environmental issues. *Organization Science*, **14**(5): 510–27.

Bansal, P. 2005. Evolving sustainably: A longitudinal study of corporate sustainable development. *Strategic Management Journal*, **26**(3): 197–218.

Bansal, P. and Clelland, I. 2004. Talking trash: Legitimacy, impression management, and unsystematic risk in the context of the natural environment. *Academy of Management Journal*, **47**(1): 93–103.

Bansal, P. and Hunter, T. 2003. Strategic explanations for the early adoption of ISO 14001. *Journal of Business Ethics*, **46**(4): 289–99.

Bansal, P. and Roth, K. 2000. Why companies go green: A model of ecological responsiveness. *Academy of Management Journal*, **43**(4): 717–36.

Barney, J.B. 1991. Firm resources and sustained competitive advantage. *Journal of Management*, **17**(1): 99–120.

Berkhout, T. and Rowlands, I.H. 2007. The voluntary adoption of green electricity by Ontario-based companies: The importance of organizational values and organizational context. *Organization & Environment*, **20**(3): 281–303.

Berrone, P. and Gomez-Meija, L.R. 2009. Environmental performance and executive compensation: An integrated agency-institutional perspective. *Academy of Management Journal*, **52**(1): 103–26.

Bies, R.J., Bartunek, J.M., Fort, T.L. and Zald, M.N. 2007. Corporations as social change agents: Individual, interpersonal, institutional, and environmental dynamics. *Academy of Management Review*, **32**(3): 788–93.

Boiral, O., Cayer, M. and Baron, C.M. 2008. The action logics of environmental leadership: A developmental perspective. *Journal of Business Ethics*, **85**: 479–99.

Bowen, F. 2002. Organizational slack and corporate greening: Broadening the debate. *British Journal of Management*, **75**(4): 97–113.

Bowen, F. 2007. Corporate social strategy: Competing views from two theories of the firm. *Journal of Business Ethics*, **75**(1): 97–113.

Branzei, O., Ursacki-Bryant, T.J., Vertinsky, I. and Zhang, W. 2004. The formation of green strategies in Chinese firms: Matching corporate environmental responses and individual principles. *Strategic Management Journal*, **25**(11): 1075–95.

Brenner, S.N. and Cochran, P. 1991. The stakeholder theory of the firm: Implications for business and society theory and research. Paper presented at the annual meeting of the International Association for Business and Society, Sundance, UT.

Brundtland Report. 1987. *Our Common Future*. Chapter 2: Towards sustainable development, available at: http://www.un-documents.net/ocf-02.htm#I; accessed 15 June 2010. Oxford: Oxford University Press.

Burt, R.S. (1992). *Structural Holes*. Cambridge, MA: Harvard University Press.

Burt, R.S. (1997). The contingent value of social capital. *Administrative Science Quarterly*, **42**(2): 339–65.

Buysse, K. and Verbeke, A. 2003. Proactive environmental strategies: A stakeholder management perspective. *Strategic Management Journal*, **24**(5): 453–70.

Campbell, J.L. 2007. Why would corporations behave in socially responsible ways? An institutional theory of corporate social responsibility. *Academy of Management Review*, **32**(3): 946–67.

Carroll, A.B. 1979. A three-dimensional conceptual model of corporate performance. *Academy of Management Review*, **4**(4): 497–505.

Chatterji, A.K., Levine, D.I. and Toffel, M.W. 2008. How well do social ratings actually measure corporate social responsibility? *Journal of Economics and Management Strategy*, **18**(1): 125–69.

Chen, Y. 2008. The driver of green innovation and green image: Green core competence. *Journal of Business Ethics*, **81**(3): 531–43.

Chertow, M.R. 2000. Industrial symbiosis: literature and taxonomy. *Annual Review of Energy and the Environment*, **25**(1): 313–37.

Child, J. 1972. Organizational structure, environment, and performance: The role of strategic choice. *Sociology*, **6**(1): 2–22.

Christmann, P. 2000. Effects of 'best practices' of environmental management on cost advantage: The role of complementary assets. *Academy of Management Journal*, **43**(4): 663–80.

Christmann, P. 2004. Multinational companies and the natural environment: Determinants of global environmental policy standardization. *Academy of Management Journal*, **47**(5): 747–60.

Clarkson, M.B.E. 1995. A stakeholder framework for analyzing and evaluating corporate social performance. *Academy of Management Review*, **20**(1): 92–117.

Coase, R. 1937. The nature of the firm. *Economica*, **4**(6): 386–405.

Cohen, B. and Winn, M.I. 2007. Market imperfections, opportunity and sustainable entrepreneurship. *Journal of Business Venturing*, **22**(1): 29–49.

Cordano, M. and Frieze, I.H. 2000. Pollution reduction preferences of US environmental managers: Applying Ajzen's theory of planned behavior. *Academy of Management Journal*, **43**(4): 627–41.

Cyert, R.M. and March, J.G. 1963. *A Behavioral Theory of the Firm*. Englewood Cliffs, NJ: Prentice Hall.

Darnall, N. and Edwards, D. 2006. Predicting the cost of environmental management system adoption: The role of capabilities, resources and ownership structure. *Strategic Management Journal*, **27**(2): 301–20.

Darnell, Carmin. 2005. Greener and cleaner? The signaling accuracy of US voluntary environmental programs. *Policy Sciences*, **38**(2–3): 71–90.

Davis, G.F. and Marquis, C. 2005. Prospects for organization theory in the early twenty-first century: Institutional fields and mechanisms. *Organization Science*, **16**(4): 332–43.

Dean, T.J. and McMullen, J.S. 2007. Toward a theory of sustainable entrepreneurship: Reducing environmental degradation through entrepreneurial action. *Journal of Business Venturing*, **22**(1): 50–76.

Delmas, M. and Keller, A. 2005. Free riding in voluntary environmental programs: case of the U.S. EPA WasteWise program. *Policy Sciences*, **38**(2–3): 91–106.

Delmas, M. and Toffel, M.W. 2004. Stakeholders and environmental management practices: An institutional framework. *Business Strategy and the Environment*, **13**(4): 209–22.

Delmas, M. and Toffel, M.W. 2008. Organizational responses to environmental demands: Opening the black box. *Strategic Management Journal*, **29**(10): 1027–55.

Del Rio, P. 2009. The empirical analysis of the determinants for environmental technological change: A research agenda. *Ecological Economics*, **68**(3): 861–78.

Den Hond, F. and De Bakker, F.G.A. 2007. Ideologically motivated activism: How activist groups influence corporate social change activities. *Academy of Management Review*, **32**(4): 901–24.

DesJardins, J. 1998. Corporate environmental responsibility. *Journal of Business Ethics*, **17**(8): 825–38.

DiMaggio, P.J. and Powell, W.W. 1983. The iron cage revisited: Institutional isomorphism and collective rationality in organizational fields. *American Sociological Review*, **48**(2): 147–60.

Donaldson, T. 1999. Making stakeholder theory whole. *Academy of Management Review*, **24**(2): 237–41.

Donaldson, T. and Preston, L.E. 1995. The stakeholder theory of the corporation: Concepts, evidence, and implications. *Academy of Management Review*, **20**(1): 65–91.

Douglas, T.J. and Judge, W.Q. 2001. Total quality management implementation and competitive advantage: The role of structural control and exploration. *Academy of Management Journal*, **44**(1): 158–69.

Dowell, G., Hart, S. and Yeung Do, B. 2000. Do corporate global environmental standards create or destroy market value? *Management Science*, **46**(8): 1059–74.

Dunlap, R. and Van Liere, K.D. 2008. The 'new environmental paradigm'. *Journal of Environmental Education*, **40**(1): 19–28.

Dutton, J.E. and Jackson, S.E. 1987. Categorizing strategic issues: links to organizational action. *Academy of Management Review*, **12**(1): 76–90.

Dyllick, T. and Hockerts, K. 2002. Beyond the business case for corporate sustainability. *Business Strategy and the Environment*, **11**(2): 130–41.

Eesley, C. and Lenox, M.J. 2006. Firm responses to secondary stakeholder action. *Strategic Management Journal*, **27**(8): 765–81.

Egri, C.P. and Herman, S. 2000. Leadership in the North American environmental sector: Values, leadership styles, and contexts of environmental leaders and their organizations. *Academy of Management Journal*, **43**(4): 571–604.

Eisenhardt, K. and Martin, J. 2000. Dynamic capabilities: What are they? *Strategic Management Journal*, **21**(10–11): 1105–21.

Elkington, J. 1998. *Cannibals with Forks: The Triple Bottom Line of 21st Century Business*. Oxford: Capstone.

Etzion, D. 2007. Research on organizations and the natural environment, 1992–present: A review. *Journal of Management*, **33**(4): 637.

Foss, N.J. 1996. Knowledge-based approaches to the theory of the firm: Some critical comments. *Organization Science*, **7**(5): 470–76.

Gargiulo, M. and Bernassi, M. (1999). The dark side of social capital. In R. Leenders and S.M. Gabbay (eds), *Corporate Social Capital and Liability*. Boston, MA: Kluwer, pp. 298–322.

Garriga, E. and Mele, D. 2004. Corporate social responsibility theories: Mapping the territory. *Journal of Business Ethics*, **53**(1–2): 51–71.

Gerde, V.W. and Logsdon, J.M. 2001. Measuring environmental performance: Use of the toxics release inventory (tri) and other US environmental databases. *Business Strategy and the Environment*, **10**(5): 269–85.

Giovannucci, D. and Ponte, S. 2005. Standards as a new form of social contract? Sustainability initiatives in the coffee industry. *Food Policy*, **30**(3): 284–301.

Gladwin, T., Kennelly, J.J. and Krause, T. 1995. Shifting paradigms for sustainable development: Implications for management theory and research. *Academy of Management Review*, **20**(4): 874–907.

Gonzalez, P. 2009. The empirical analysis of the determinants for environmental technological change: A research agenda. *Ecological Economics*, **68**(3): 861–78.

Gopinath, C. 2008. *Globalization*. Thousand Oaks, CA: Sage Publications, Inc.

Greenwood, R., Suddaby, R. and Hinings, C.R. 2002. Theorizing change: The role of professional associations in the transformation of institutionalized fields. *Academy of Management Journal*, **45**(1): 58–80.

Hamilton, J.T. 1995. Pollution as news: Media and stock market reactions to the toxics release inventory data. *Journal of Environmental Economics*, **28**(1): 98–113.

Harrison, J.S and Freeman, R.E. 1999. Stakeholders, social responsibility, and performance: Empirical evidence and theoretical perspectives. *Academy of Management Journal*, **42**(5): 479–85.

Hart, S.L. 1995. A natural-resource-based view of the firm. *Academy of Management Review*, **20**(4): 969–1014.

Hart, S.L. and Ahuja, G. 1996. Does it pay to be green? An empirical examination of the relationship between emission reduction and firm performance. *Business Strategy and the Environment*, **5**(1): 30–37.

Helfat C.E. 1997. Know-how and asset complementarity and dynamic capability accumulation. *Strategic Management Journal*, **18**(5): 339–60.

Helfat, C.E. and Peteraf, M.A. 2003. The dynamic resource-based view. *Strategic Management Journal*, **24**(10): 997–1010.

Henriques, I. and Sadorsky, P. 1999. The relationship between environmental commitment and managerial perceptions of stakeholder performance. *Academy of Management Journal*, **42**(1): 87–99.

Hilliard, R. 2004. Conflicting views: Neoclassical, Porterian, and evolutionary approaches to the analysis of the environmental regulation of industrial activity. *Journal of Economic Issues*, **30**(2): 509–17.

Hillman, A.J. and Keim, G.D. 2001. Shareholder value, stakeholder management, and social issues: What's the bottom line? *Strategic Management Journal*, **22**(2): 125–39.

Hoffman, A.J. 1999. Institutional evolution and change: Environmentalism and the US chemical industry. *Academy of Management Journal*, **42**(1): 351–71.

Hoffman, A.J. and Ocasio, W. 2001. Not all events are attended equally: Toward a middle-range theory of industry attention to external events. *Organization Science*, **12**(4): 414–34.

Horbach, J.J. 2008. Determinants of environmental innovation: New evidence from German panel data sources. *Research Policy*, **37**(1): 163–73.

Hull, C.E. and Rothenberg, S. 2008. Firm performance: The interactions of corporate social performance with innovation and industry differentiation. *Strategic Management Journal*, **29**(7): 781–9.

Husted, B.W. and Allen, D.B. 2006. Corporate social responsibility in the multinational enterprise: Strategic and institutional approaches. *Journal of International Business Studies*, **37**(6): 838–49.

Ilinitch, A.Y. and Schaltegger, S.C. 1995. Developing a green business portfolio. *Long Range Planning*, **28**(2): 29–38.

Jackson, S.E. and Dutton, J.E. 1988. Discerning threats and opportunities. *Administrative Science Quarterly*, **33**(3): 370–87.

Jaffe, A.B., Newell, R.G. and Stavins, R.N. 2005. A tale of two market failures: Technology and environmental policy. *Ecological Economics*, **54**(2–3): 164–74.

Jennings, P.D. and Zandbergen, P.A. 1995. Ecologically sustainable organizations: An institutional approach. *Academy of Management Review*, **20**(4): 1015–52.

Jiang, R.J. and Bansal, P. 2003. Seeing the need for ISO 14001. *Journal of Management Studies*, **40**(4): 1047–67.

Judge, W.Q. and Douglas, T.J. 1998. Performance implications of incorporating natural environmental issues into the strategic planning process: An empirical assessment. *Journal of Management Studies*, **35**(2): 241–62.

Kassinis, G. and Vafeas, N. 2002. Corporate boards and outside stakeholders as determinants of environmental litigation. *Strategic Management Journal*, **23**(5): 399–415.

Kassinis, G. and Vafeas, N. 2006. Stakeholder pressures and environmental performance. *Academy of Management Journal*, **49**(1): 145–59.

Khanna, M. and Anton, W.R. 2002. Corporate environmental management: Regulatory and market-based incentives. *Land Economics*, **78**(4): 539–58.

King, A. 2007. Cooperation between corporations and environmental groups: A transaction cost perspective. *Academy of Management Review*, **32**(3): 889–900.

King, A.A. and Lenox, M.J. 2000. Industry self-regulation without sanctions: The chemical industry's responsible care program. *Academy of Management Journal*, **43**(4): 698–716.

King, A.A. and Lenox, M.J. 2002. Exploring the locus of profitable pollution reduction. *Management Science*, **48**(2): 289–99.

King, A.A., Lenox, M.J. and Terlaak, A. 2005. The strategic use of decentralized institutions: Exploring certification with the ISO 14001 management standard. *Academy of Management Journal*, **48**(6): 1091–106.

Kogut, B. and Zander, U. 1992. Knowledge of the firm, combinative capabilities, and the replication of technology. *Organization Science*, **3**(3): 383–97.

Kolk, A. and Pinkse, J. 2008. A perspective on multinational enterprises and climate change: Learning from 'An Inconvenient Truth'? *Journal of International Business Studies*, **39**(8): 1359–78.

Konar, S. and Cohen, M.A. 2001. Does the market value environmental performance? *Review of Economics and Statistics*, **83**(2): 281–9.

Larson, A.L. 2000. Sustainable innovation through an entrepreneurship lens. *Business Strategy and the Environment*, **9**(5): 304–17.

Laszlo, C., Sherman, D., Whalen, J. and Ellison, J. 2005. How stakeholder value contributes to competitive advantage. *Journal of Corporate Citizenship*, **20**: 65–76.

Lee, M.P. 2008. A review of the theories of corporate social responsibility: Its evolutionary path and the road ahead. *International Journal of Management Reviews*, **10**(1): 53–73.

Lewis, D. 2003. NGOs, organizational culture, and institutional sustainability. *Annals of the American Academy of Political and Social Science*, **590**(1): 212–26.

Lewis, M.W. 2000. Exploring paradox: Toward a more comprehensive guide. *Academy of Management Review*, **25**(4): 760–76.

Lynes, J.K. and Andrachuk, M. 2008. Motivations for corporate social and environmental responsibility: A case study of Scandinavian Airlines. *Journal of International Management*, **14**(4): 377–90.

Maguire, S. and Hardy, C. 2006. The emergence of new global institutions: A discursive perspective. *Organization Studies*, **27**(1): 7–29.

Mair, J. and Marti, I. 2006. Social entrepreneurship research: A source of explanation, prediction, and delight. *Journal of World Business*, **41**(1): 36–44.

Majumdar, S.K. and Marcus, A.A. 2001. Rules versus discretion: The productivity consequences of flexible regulation. *Academy of Management Journal*, **44**(1): 170–79.

Marcus, A.A. and Anderson, M.H. 2006. A general dynamic capability: Does it propagate business and social competencies in the retail food industry? *Journal of Management Studies*, **43**(1): 19–46.

Marcus, A. and Geffen, D. 1998. The dialectics of competency acquisition: Pollution prevention in electric generation. *Strategic Management Journal*, **19**(12): 1145–68.

Margolis, J.D. and Walsh, J.P. 2003. Misery loves companies: Rethinking social initiatives by business. *Administrative Science Quarterly*, **48**(2): 268–305.

Matten, D. and Crane, A. 2005. Corporate citizenship: Toward an extended theoretical conceptualization. *Academy of Management Review*, **30**(1): 166–79.

Matten, D. and Moon, J. 2008. 'Implicit' and 'explicit' CSR: A conceptual framework for a comparative understanding of corporate social responsibility. *Academy of Management Review*, **33**(2): 404–24.

Mattingly, J.E. and Berman, S.L. 2006. Measurement of corporate social action: Discovering taxonomy in the Kinder Lydenburg Domini ratings data. *Business & Society*, **45**(1): 20–46.

McWilliams, A. and Siegel, D. 2000. Corporate social responsibility and financial performance: Correlation or misspecification? *Strategic Management Journal*, **21**(5): 603–9.

McWilliams, A. and Siegel, D. 2001. Corporate social responsibility: A theory of the firm perspective. *Academy of Management Review*, **26**(1): 117–27.

Meyer, J. and Rowan, B. 1977. Institutional organizations: Formal structure as myth and ceremony. *American Journal of Sociology*, **83**(2): 340–63.

Nehrt, C. 1998. Maintainability of first mover advantages when environmental regulations differ between countries. *Academy of Management Review*, **23**(1): 77–97.

Ocasio, W. 1997. Towards an attention-based view of the firm. *Journal of Strategic Management*, **18** (Summer Special): 187–206.

Oetzel, J. and Doh, J.P. 2009. MNEs and development: A review and reconceptualization. *Journal of World Business*, **44**(2): 108–20.

Orlitzky, M., Schmidt, F.L. and Rynes, S.L. 2003. Corporate social and financial performance: A meta-analysis. *Organization Studies*, **24**(3): 403–41.

Parker, M. and Pearson, G. 2005. Capitalism and its regulation: A dialogue on business and ethics. *Journal of Business Ethics*, **60**(1): 91–101.

Penrose, E.T. 1959. *The Theory of Growth of the Firm*. London: Basil Blackwell.

Peteraf, M.A. 1993. The cornerstones of competitive advantage: A resource-based approach. *Strategic Management Journal*, **14**(3): 179–91.

Potoski, M. and Prakash, A. 2005. Green clubs and voluntary governance: ISO 14001 and firms' regulatory compliance. *American Journal of Political Science*, **49**(2): 235–48.

Reinstaller, A. 2005. Policy entrepreneurship in the co-evolution of institutions, preferences and technology: Comparing the diffusion of totally chlorine-free pulp bleaching technologies in the US and Sweden. *Research Policy*, **34**(9): 1366–84.

Roberts, J. 2003. The manufacture of corporate social responsibility. *Organization*, **10**: 249–65.

Rose, J.M. 2007. Corporate directors and social responsibility: Ethics versus shareholder value. *Journal of Business Ethics*, **73**(3): 319–31.

Rowlands, I.H. 2001. The Kyoto Protocol's 'Clean Development Mechanism': A sustainability assessment. *Third World Quarterly*, **22**(5): 795–811.

Rudra, N. 2002. Globalization and the decline of the welfare state in less-developed countries. *International Organization*, **56**(2): 411–45.

Rugman, A.M. and Verbeke, A. 1998. Corporate strategies and environmental regulations: An organizing framework. *Strategic Management Journal*, **19**(4): 363–75.

Russo, M.V. and Fouts, P.A. 1997. A resource-based perspective on corporate environmental performance and profitability. *Academy of Management Journal*, **40**(3): 534–59.

Russo, M.V. and Harrison, N.S. 2005. Organizational design and environmental performances: Clues from the electronics industry. *Academy of Management Journal*, **48**(4): 582–93.

Scherer, A.G. and Palazzo, G. 2007. Toward a political conception of corporate responsibility: business and society seen from a Habermasian perspective. *Academy of Management Review*, **32**(4): 1096–120.

Scott, W.R. 1992. *Organizations: Rational, Natural, and Open Systems*. Englewood Cliffs, NJ: Prentice Hall.

Sharma, S. 2000. Managerial interpretations and organizational context as predictors of corporate choice of environmental strategy. *Academy of Management Journal*, **43**(4): 681–97.

Sharma, S. and Henriques, I. 2005. Stakeholder influences on sustainability practices in the Canadian forest products industry. *Strategic Management Journal*, **26**(2): 159–80.

Sharma, S. and Nguan, O. 1999. The biotechnology industry and strategies of biodiversity conservation: The influence of managerial interpretations and risk propensity. *Business Strategy and the Environment*, **8**(1): 46–61.

Sharma, S. and Vredenburg, H. 1998. Proactive corporate environmental strategy and the development of competitively valuable organizational capabilities. *Strategic Management Journal*, **19**(8): 729–53.

Sharma, S., Pablo, A.L. and Vredenburg, H. 1999. Corporate environmental responsiveness strategies: The importance of issue interpretation and organizational context. *Journal of Applied Behavioral Science*, **35**(1): 87–108.

Shrivastava, P. 1995. The role of corporations in achieving ecological sustainability. *Academy of Management Review*, **20**(4): 939–60.

Siegel, D.S. 2009. Green management matters only if it yields more green: An economic/strategic perspective. *Academy of Management Perspectives*, **23**(3): 5–16.

Sreekumar, T.T. and Parayil, G. 2002. Contentions and contradictions of tourism as development option: The case of Kerala, India. *Third World Quarterly*, **23**(3): 529–48.

Starik, M. and Marcus, A.A. 2000. Introduction to the special research forum on the management of organizations in the natural environment: A field emerging from multiple paths, with many challenges ahead. *Academy of Management Journal*, **43**(4): 539–46.

Starik, M. and Rands, G.P. 1995. Weaving an integrated web: Multilevel and multisystem perspectives of ecologically sustainable organizations. *Academy of Management Review*, **20**(4): 908–35.

Starkey, K. and Crane, A. 2003. Toward green narrative: Management and the evolutionary epic. *Academy of Management Review*, **28**(2): 220–37.

Swanson, D.L. 1999. Toward an integrative theory of business and society: A research strategy for corporate social performance. *Academy of Management Review*, **24**(3): 506–21.

Szekely, F. and Knirsch, M. 2005. Responsible leadership and corporate social responsibility: Metrics for sustainable performance. *European Management Journal*, **23**(6): 628–47.

Teece, D.J., Pisano, G.P. and Shuen, A. 1997. Dynamic capabilities and strategic management. *Strategic Management Journal*, **18**(1): 509–33.

Teegan, H., Doh, J.P. and Vachani, S. 2004. The importance of nongovernmental organizations (NGOs) in global governance and value creation: An international business research agenda. *Journal of International Business Studies*, **35**(6): 463–83.

Tello, S.F. and Yoon, E. 2008. Examining drivers of sustainable innovation. *Journal of International Business Strategy*, **8**(3): 164–9.

Tenbrunsel, A.E., Wade-Benzoni, K.A., Messick, D.M. and Bazerman, M.H. 2000. Understanding the influence of environmental standards on judgments and choices. *Academy of Management Journal*, **43**(5): 854–66.

Terlaak, A. 2007. Order without law? The role of certified management standards in shaping socially desired firm behaviors. *Academy of Management Review*, **32**(3): 968–85.

Thomas, J.B. and McDaniel, R.R. 1990. Interpreting strategic issues: Effects of strategy and the information processing structure of top management teams. *Academy of Management Journal*, **33**(2): 286–306.

Thomson, D. and Khare, A. 2008. Carbon capture and storage (CCS) deployment – can Canada capitalize on experience? *Journal of Technology Management and Innovation*, **3**(4): 111–18.

Toffel, M.W. and Marshall, J.D. 2004. Improving environmental performance assessment: A comparative analysis of weighting methods used to evaluate chemical release inventories. *Journal of Industrial Ecology*, **8**(1–2): 143–72.

Van Alphen, K., Van Ruijven, J., Kasa, S., Hekkert, M. and Turkenburg,W. 2009. The performance of the Norwegian carbon dioxide, capture and storage innovation system. *Energy Policy*, **37**(2): 43–55.

Wagner, M. 2007. On the relationship between environmental management, environmental innovation and patenting: Evidence from German manufacturing firms. *Research Policy*, **36**(10): 1587–602.

Wartick, S.L. and Cochran, P.L. 1985. The evolution of the corporate social performance model. *Academy of Management Review*, **10**(4): 758–69.

Weidenbaum, M. 2009. Who will guard the guardians? The social responsibility of NGOs. *Journal of Business Ethics*, **87**(1): 147–55.

Wernerfelt, B. 1984. A resource-based view of the firm. *Strategic Management Journal*, **5**(2): 171–80.

Wiklund, J. and Shepherd, D. 2003. Knowledge-based resources, entrepreneurial orientation, and the performance of small and medium-sized businesses. *Strategic Management Journal*, **24**(13): 1307–14.

Williamson, O.E. 1975. *Markets and Hierarchies: Analysis and Antitrust Implications*. New York: The Free Press.

Williamson, O.E. 1985. *The Economic Institutions of Capitalism*, New York: The Free Press.

Williamson, O.E. 1991. Strategizing, economizing, and economic organization. *Strategic Management Journal*, **12**(52): 75–94.

Wood, D.J. 1991. Corporate social performance revisited. *Academy of Management Review*, **16**(4): 691–718.

Wry, T.E. 2009. Does business and society scholarship matter to society? Pursuing a normative agenda with critical realism and neoinstitutional theory. *Journal of Business Ethics*, **89**(2): 151–71.

3 MNCs' social, ethical and legal responsibilities (corporate social responsibility)*

Bobby Banerjee, Timo Busch, Tom Cooper, Daina Mazutis and Josephine Stomp

OVERVIEW BY TOM COOPER

Corporate Social Responsibility

The Corporate Social Responsibility (CSR) group started with asking, what are the big questions that we need to be examining in the field? Addressing these led to a discussion about the current state of the CSR literature and existing gaps. In our overview, which follows, we are more interested in identifying rather than understanding the effects of the gaps. We believe that identification of the gaps in the CSR literature is the more pressing concern for academic researchers and is needed to fully develop the field.

Themes in the Academic Corporate Social Responsibility Literature

The CSR group identified four broad themes that describe the CSR literature. The first was rhetoric versus reality in how organizations are managing CSR. The second theme related to how the academic literature views CSR from both a negative and positive standpoint. The third theme emerging was about changing the 'usual' in 'business as usual'. Lastly, a theme emerged around the need for a holistic understanding of what CSR is, its implications for management, as well as future trends.

Figure 3.1 depicts our view of the CSR field and gaps in the literature. The figure is explained below.

Theme 1 – rhetoric vs. reality
In our review, the dichotomy of rhetoric versus reality was the initial theme that defines the CSR academic field. Most of the CSR academic literature

---

* Facilitators: Oana Branzei and Patricia Gonçalves Vidal.

Moving forward the field

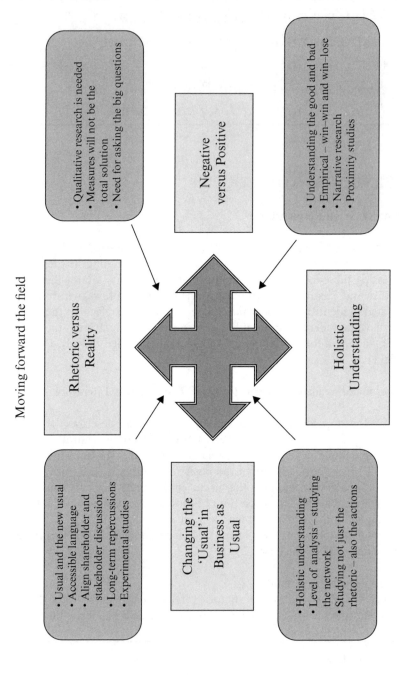

Qualitative research is needed
• Measures will not be the total solution
• Need for asking the big questions

Negative versus Positive

• Understanding the good and bad
• Empirical – win–win and win–lose
• Narrative research
• Proximity studies

Rhetoric versus Reality

Holistic Understanding

• Usual and the new usual
• Accessible language
• Align shareholder and stakeholder discussion
• Long-term repercussions
• Experimental studies

Changing the 'Usual' in Business as Usual

• Holistic understanding
• Level of analysis – studying the network
• Studying not just the rhetoric – also the actions

Figure 3.1 CSR literature themes and gaps

has focused on how corporations are accountable as well as developing a sense of what is 'accountability'. However, in order to understand and move the literature forward within the CSR field, there is a need to address the lack of quality qualitative empirical research. Specifically, there is an absence of longitudinal studies describing how firms and managers are managing CSR. Only through gaining a full appreciation of the issue of time and how it affects the management of CSR, can there truly be an understanding of what is rhetoric and reality in the CSR literature.

The lack of rich, quality, empirical research lends itself to the predominance of rhetoric. Essentially, we believe that companies and managers are more focused on telling researchers what they believe is consistent with current trends in the CSR field (rhetoric) rather than explaining what is really happening (reality). Focusing on longitudinal studies, we believe can assist researchers in the better understanding of what reality is in the CSR field.

It is important to note that in reviewing the literature, we believe that the trend towards rhetoric is not necessary negative. Instead, rhetoric is a necessary starting point in moving the field forward. Understanding and reiterating concepts as well as the prose that defines the CSR field needs to be in place before quality empirical research can take place. Essentially we believe that triangulation and quantification can wait while the big questions are addressed. The result of waiting may be a paucity of published CSR-related articles in the top-tier journals that demand triangulation and quantification. As a group, we believe that rhetoric is fundamental to advancing the CSR field and it is important that the concepts, theories and approaches are more fully articulated and communicated.

To become a mature area of academic research, the area of CSR must begin to answer the big theory questions. These questions are: To what extent do we have ceremonial compliance in CSR? How does government fit into stakeholder theory? How does institutional theory explain how organizations manage CSR? Can institutional theory deconstruct CSR? Bringing in concepts and theories from other disciplines should help in addressing the big theory questions so that the CSR field may advance.

Theme 2 – negative vs. positive scholarship
Another theme we found was the notion of negative versus positive scholarship. In reviewing the literature, we believe that there is difficulty for researchers in identifying and understanding the issues that surround CSR. This difficulty is further complicated by a desire to take either a pessimistic or 'cheerleading' role when empirically researching CSR.

In positive scholarship, researchers are interested in the companies that are doing well. Some may see this as cheerleading rather than understanding the importance and relevance of positive scholarship. For example, research on organizations that publish environmental reports to enhance their legitimacy would be indicative of positive research. Yet, as researchers we know that there is always the potential for green-washing in environmental reports. Ultimately there may be no need to differentiate between positive and negative scholarship – the two may co-exist.

Generally, most of the CSR research was extremely pessimistic and cynical. Yet it was limited in its description, which led to criticism without validity. Ultimately, researchers and practitioners do not understand the difference between the good and bad in this field and this is a significant gap in the literature.

Regardless of whether it is positive or negative scholarship, good empirical research is needed to differentiate between the good and bad organizations, concepts, theories and variables in the CSR field. The development of this differentiation can be assisted through researching both 'win–win' as well as 'win–lose' situations for organizations and management.

Some of these 'win–win' and 'win–lose' situations may be explored through narrative rather than measured empirical research. Narratives push researchers toward explaining how CSR is being managed through policies, procedures and reports. To advance the field as well as gain an understanding of good and bad, empirical measures are not sufficient. If measures are used, they need to be grounded in an explicit understanding of how they are managed. For example, there is a need for more cultural understanding as well as regulation and politics in the development of approaches to CSR. It will be difficult to empirically research these approaches to CSR, yet this difficulty does not excuse the gap in the literature.

Theme 3 – changing the usual
The third major theme that emerges within the CSR literature is in 'changing the usual'. We believe that there is a need to understand the 'usual' as well as what will emerge as the new 'usual' as the CSR field develops. For example, environmental management is seen as an approach that most companies use in addressing CSR. Yet environmental management may be just one element of a wider approach to environmental governance that organizations must embrace if they are to advance their approach to CSR. Ultimately, researchers assume what the 'usual' is and do not have a good grasp on how business approaches the 'usual'. Obtaining a better understanding of the usual and how it evolves is necessary to advance academic research within the CSR field. We need to know what the usual CSR actions are that companies undertake and how they lead to better approaches and strategies.

An analogy is to the total quality management (TQM) field. Originally a technical field, TQM is now a commonly understood term in the management literature. It has entered a mature stage in its development.

Executives, consultants, regulators and other stakeholders need to understand the language of CSR so that it has a wider audience beyond keenly interested academics. Ensuring the language is understood by a wide spectrum of stakeholders is consistent with how TQM has been able to develop as a field and will be necessary to advance CSR and address gaps in the literature.

Understanding the 'new usual' we believe will also help in aligning the stakeholder and shareholder discussion in the academic field. In our review, the academic literature is overly preoccupied with the stakeholder and shareholder discussion as exemplified in the debate around corporate social performance (CSP) vs. CSR. We believe that this preoccupation with stakeholder vs. shareholder needs to be addressed to further the academic literature. Ultimately, researchers may be getting into a vicious circle because CSP and CSR are difficult concepts to research. We may be limiting the field by focusing on CSP.

Studying the long-term repercussions of CSR is an approach to the stakeholder vs. shareholder issue. In utilizing longitudinal studies, researchers can examine if companies are making a difference over time, thus better understanding the impact of CSR. Another approach to better understanding where and how CSR is making a difference is experimental studies and simulations. Ultimately in experimental studies we can shame people into doing the new 'usual' thing, thus changing 'business as usual'. Through simulations, we can understand where organizations and management can benefit from managing different elements of CSR. The lack of experimental and simulation studies points to a gap in the literature.

Theme 4 – holistic approach to CSR
The final theme that emerged from the literature was whether a holisitic understanding of CSR is needed. Taking a holistic approach may be difficult for academic researchers. For example, CSR may be dissimilar in different industries such as the chemical industry. However, refusing to recognize the different contextual approaches to CSR may mean gaps developing in cross-industry and cross-cultural studies.

Ultimately, in examining some of the concepts underpinning the CSR field such as governance and citizenship, there is a need to get a better understanding of the fundamental concepts of CSR. Understanding the policies, procedures and controls that accompany a management approach to CSR is a definite gap.

Since the lack of understanding of what really underpins CSR and how it is managed is evident in the literature, the level of analysis becomes another issue. Researchers need to study not just the rhetoric but also the actions as well as those actors affected but not involved in the decision-making. In taking a more holistic approach to understanding CSR as well as how concepts are inter-related, this should address some of the major gaps in the academic literature.

REVIEWS BY BOBBY BANERJEE

Margolis, J.D. and Walsh, J.P. 2003. Misery loves companies: Rethinking social initiatives by business. *Administrative Science Quarterly*, **48(2): 268–305.**

In this paper the authors provide a critical analysis of research on corporate social responsibility by focusing on two themes: (1) empirical research going back to the last 30 years that has attempted to establish a relationship between corporate social initiatives, and (2) financial performance and an appraisal of developments in stakeholder theory. The authors argue that there is an inherent and unresolved tension between calls for corporations to address the social ills facing the world and the economic imperatives that firms must pursue in order to prosper. The modern corporation has evolved in its current form as a result of particular economic, political and social circumstances that have entrenched the economic notion of a firm as a nexus of contracts. The contractarian approach assumes that different actors enter into contracts with the sole aim of wealth creation. Any attempts to pursue 'social' goals by firms are bound to come up against constraints arising from the goals of a contractarian view of the firm where social initiatives could be seen as both misappropriation and misallocation of organizational resources.

In an attempt to overcome the tension between economic and social interests, scholars developed the notion of organizational stakeholders. Stakeholder theory was an attempt to make explicit the social role of organizations and instead of conceptualizing the firm as a nexus of contracts between economic actors, the corporation was seen as an entity that balanced the needs of a variety of internal and external stakeholders, of which society in general was also seen as a legitimate stakeholder. However, despite normative attempts to integrate stakeholder interests it is the instrumental approach that has prevailed. Corporate social responsibility in the framework of stakeholder theory is limited to win–win situations starting with the assumption that it makes good business sense and enhances shareholder value. Thus, as Margolis and Walsh (2003) point out, the entirety of empirical research on the economic performance–social performance link, and indeed all of the conceptual research on stakeholder theory, actually serves to authenticate the economic contractarian model because it accepts its assumptions and does not pose an alternate view.

There is an assumption that a corporation that takes into account the needs of all its stakeholders will also be successful in traditional performance criteria. This is a proposition that has received little empirical support. Margolis and Walsh (2003) in a study of 127 empirical studies conducted during 1972–2002 measuring the relationship between corporate social performance and corporate financial performance found that about half the studies reported a positive relationship. The research findings are far from convincing, however, and recent reviews have pointed out serious shortcomings ranging from sampling problems, measurement issues, omission of controls, and more significantly, lack of explanatory theory linking CSR with financial performance (McWilliams and Siegel, 2000; Orlitzky et al., 2003). However, the authors found little evidence of a *negative* relationship. In other words there is no evidence to state that corporate social responsibility can harm the wealth-generating ability of business firms, which should lead to alleviating concerns about diminishing shareholder value.

To summarize, we can discern three approaches to stakeholder theory in the literature: the shareholder value perspective, which sees stakeholder theory as a 'dangerous distortion of business principles', the stakeholder value perspective aimed at making corporations more socially responsible by balancing the needs of different stakeholders and the managerial perspective, a 'middle way' that identifies salient stakeholders in order to manage them efficiently. Thus, the primary approach, despite some normative concessions, remains avowedly instrumental whereby theoretical approaches focus on reconciling corporate social initiatives with the economic view of the firm.

Margolis and Walsh (2003, p. 284), while acknowledging this drawback, call for a normative theory of the firm where the role of management scholars is to identify the 'principles and guidelines for managing trade-offs, rather than assert, deny or reconcile competing legitimacy claims of stakeholders'. However, they do not address the political and power dynamics that govern the process of developing principles for managing trade-offs. The normative core of stakeholder theory is said to be a driver of corporate social performance and once managers accept their obligations to stakeholders and recognize their legitimacy, the corporation is well on its way to achieving its moral principles (Clarkson, 1995). This is a simplistic argument that fails to recognize the inability of a framework to represent different realities and the effects of using a single lens to view issues such as legitimacy and responsibility.

Proponents of stakeholder theory claim that corporate social performance can be evaluated based on the management of a corporation's relationships with its stakeholders. The fact that social performance needs to be 'managed', implies that, as is done with business ethics, it is deployed as a strategy designed to benefit the corporation. Who decides what is socially appropriate? Who assesses it?

Nevertheless, preoccupation with justifying corporate social initiatives on the grounds that it leads to better financial performance rather than resolving the tension between economic and social good serves to sidestep the issue. Margolis and Walsh argue that instead of avoiding the tension by focusing on the economic aspects of social initiatives, the tension between the economic and social can serve as a new source of ideas for theory development. The authors adopt a pragmatic approach in resolving the tension – instead of focusing efforts on trying to find a link between social and financial performance, they call for more research on the actual long-term impacts of corporate social initiatives. What have been the beneficial or damaging consequences of particular CSR initiatives? Have the espoused social outcomes been achieved? In this approach, normative concerns are put on temporary hold as the outcomes of corporate social initiatives are first assessed. Rather than manage competing claims for legitimacy among stakeholders, Margolis and Walsh call for descriptive research to examine how corporations respond to social issues and the outcomes of CSR initiatives. This would lay the foundation for a normative analysis arising from philosophical perspectives on ethics and social justice. The descriptive approach will generate narratives on how corporations are responding to social issues while the normative approach will generate debates on how they should respond based on normative principles that govern societies. The authors then proceed to outline their descriptive and normative research agenda to develop a normative theory of the firm.

References

Clarkson, M.B.E. 1995. A stakeholder framework for analyzing and evaluating corporate social performance. *Academy of Management Review*, **20**(1): 92–117.
McWilliams, A. and Siegel, D. 2000. Corporate social responsibility and financial performance: Correlation or misspecification? *Strategic Management Journal*, **21**(5): 603–9.
Orlitzky, M., Schmidt, F.L. and Rynes, S.L. 2003. Corporate social and financial performance: A meta-analysis. *Organization Studies*, **24**(3): 403–41.

Roberts, J. 2003. The manufacture of corporate social responsibility. *Organization*, 10(2): 249–65.

In this paper, Roberts draws on philosophical insights from the work of Levinas, particularly in how the construction of ethical subjectivities through 'reflexive encrustation' of the self and 'denuding of the self' creates particular notions of 'responsibility for my neighbor'. Roberts critiques contemporary forms of CSR based on these alternative paths for the self. At one level, CSR discourses can be criticized for being just good public relations that creates a good appearance for the corporation without changing its conduct in any way. In the guise of promoting itself as a good corporate citizen, CSR can weaken ethical sensibilities while promoting a business as usual agenda.

Roberts argues that to promote a more meaningful version of business ethics, we need to understand how business and ethics became separate aspects in the first place. Neoclassical economics and agency theory created particular conceptions of the 'individual' as an opportunistic utility maximizer whose logical conclusion led to social relations that were fundamentally competitive where at best there could be moments of calculated cooperation when reciprocal self-interests coincide (p. 251). In this framework ethics is good for business because 'ethics pays'. Roberts develops the notion of corporate sensibility in an attempt to distinguish between substance and imagery, between CSR realities and glossy reports. Ethics will remain an individual matter however the construction of the appearance of ethics. What Roberts calls the 'ethics of narcissus' results in different forms of CSR.

In Levinas's formulation, ethics are not located 'within being' but 'otherwise than being', marking a separation of the self from its social context. Ethics is not just about making a choice but is always already affecting us in our sensibility. Self-identity and subjectivity are constituted by the other and 'comes to us from the outside in the assignation of responsibility for my neighbor' (ibid.). Levinas's arguments are admittedly complex but one of the interesting outcomes is that because ethical capacities of human beings are 'grounded in our corporeal sensibility' it is the antithesis of the ethics in economics argument where the question is not how to get ethics back into business but instead to examine how ethical sensibilities in business play out or how they become 'encrusted'. In some ways the implications of this conceptualization of ethics is consistent with Margolis and Walsh's (2003) call for a more pragmatic and descriptive approach to what CSR actually does before building a normative argument to assess its consequences.

Roberts discusses how the categories created by accounting (costs, profits, return on capital) are ways to 'discipline our self' in an attempt to construct a lens for others to see and judge our conduct. This 'narcissistic preoccupation' (p. 255) in the context of CSR gives rise to codes of conduct, mission statements, environmental and social reports, in addition to conventional financial statements as well as engagement in 'stakeholder dialogue'. Roberts argues that developments in environmental and social accountability has little to do with ethics per se but has more to do with the creation of new forms of corporate self-image or identity – 'a demand to be seen to be not only powerful but also good' (p. 256).

While corporate codes of conduct, environmental and social reports can be seen as increasing transparency they can also lead to a displacement of responsibility from the corporation to its employees who in the context of CSR must also be seen to be efficient and ethical. These new forms of visibility have more to do with the need to be seen as ethical rather than any radical change in operating behavior.

Roberts' critique of stakeholder dialogue exposes the shortcomings of contemporary theoretical frameworks that assess stakeholder salience (Mitchell et al., 1997) where issues of power are inadequately theorized. Corporations engage with stakeholders who tend to have an impact on public perceptions of the corporate body. Stakeholders that are disempowered by and most vulnerable to corporate activity are not in a position to enter into 'dialogue' with corporations. Thus, mechanisms like 'triple bottom line' accounting do little to address the interests of certain stakeholders and instead revert into the business as usual mode. These 'ethical' accounting measures focus on what can be easily quantified and measured and the 'social' almost always tends to be undervalued by a separation of the environment and the social from the economic. The lenses of accounting disciplinary mechanisms enable a 'seeing robbed of sensibility' (p. 257).

Thus, corporate codes of conduct and reporting mechanisms manufacture an appearance of goodness. Unless these mechanisms are accompanied by genuine dialogue with marginalized and vulnerable stakeholder groups, CSR will tend to serve corporate not societal interests.

References

Margolis, J.D. and Walsh, J.P. 2003. Misery loves companies: Rethinking social initiatives by business. *Administrative Science Quarterly*, **48**(2): 268–305.

Mitchell, R., Agle, B. and Wood, D. 1997. Toward a theory of stakeholder identification and salience: Defining the principle of who and what really counts. *Academy of Management Review*, **22**(4): 853–86.

Banerjee, S.B. 2008. Corporate social responsibility: The good, the bad and the ugly. *Critical Sociology*, 34(1): 51–79.

This paper provides a historical overview of the emergence of the modern corporation and traces the shifting power dynamics that resulted in the creation of the identity of the corporate body as an 'artificial person' with legal rights. The transition of the early corporation in the eighteenth century chartered by the state to serve public interests to its contemporary form as a nexus of contracts was an outcome of power relations between business, governments and societal actors. One of the consequences of the freeing of corporations from government and societal control was that CSR became a discretionary activity. The paper argues that despite the positive spin portrayed by CSR discourses, CSR is defined by narrow business interests and serves to curtail the interests of external stake-holders. CSR discourses represent an ideological movement that legitimizes and consolidates the power of large corporations.

The social role of corporations is defined by efficiency and legitimacy arguments. The corporation's legitimacy arises from its economic role as a provider of goods and services. But the efficiency–legitimacy dichotomy is problematic because legitimacy becomes subordinate to efficiency because the terms of legitimacy are discursively produced and defined by economic efficiency criteria. CSR and stakeholder engagement are ways that corporations can enhance their legitimacy. However, whereas CSR may have positive outcomes for corporations, the consequences of CSR practices for societal welfare are less clear because the terms of engagement are dictated by corporate, not societal interests.

The paper examines current discourses on sustainability to show the corporate capture of the environmental movement. As corporations came under increasing pressure to address environmental concerns, they eagerly embraced the discourse of sustainable development and succeeded in shifting the stated aim of planetary sustainability to organizational sustainability. For instance, the Dow Jones Sustainability Group Index defined a sustainable corporation as one 'that aims at increasing long-term shareholder value by integrating economic, environmental and social growth opportunities into its corporate and business strategies'. In this framework environmental and social issues can be integrated into corporate strategy only if they present growth opportunities. Thus, the assumption is that new technologies can lead to market expansion; the future of nature becomes contingent on the logic of markets (Shiva, 2001).

Arguing that focusing on sustainability at the level of the corporation will produce limited outcomes, the paper uses insights from Foucault's work on disciplinary power and governmentality to show how a particular corporate rationality is generated at the level of the political economy. A combination of institutional and discursive power creates particular notions of progress, development and sustainability that are reinforced by the policies of supranational institutions like the World Bank, International Monetary Fund and the World Trade Organization. In this framework, market and corporate interests tend to be privileged over community interests. For example, the paper describes how the imposition of a global intellectual property rights regime on biological resources like agricultural products and seeds with the backing of institutional and corporate interests results in disempowerment and dispossession of thousands of rural farmers in the Third World.

The paper argues that focusing on the individual corporation as the unit of analysis can only produce limited results and serves to create an organizational enclosure around corporate social responsibility. For any radical revision to occur, a more critical approach to organization theory is required and new questions need to be raised not only about the ecological and social sustainability of business corporations, but of the political economy itself. Radical revisions at this level can only occur if there is a shift in thinking at a macro-level. There is a need to open up new spaces and provide new frameworks for organization–stakeholder dialogues as well as critically examine the dynamics of the relationships between corporations, NGOs, governments, community groups and funding agencies.

Reference

Shiva, V. 2001. *Protect or Plunder: Understanding Intellectual Property Rights*. London: Zed Books.

REVIEWS BY TIMO BUSCH

Agle, B.R., Donaldson, T., Freeman, R.E., Jensen, M.C., Mitchell, R.K. and Wood, D.J. 2008. Dialogue: Toward superior stakeholder theory. *Business Ethics Quarterly*, **18(2): 153–90.**

This article is based on an All-Academy symposium at the 2007 AOM in Philadelphia. In the aftermath of the AOM, the participants, namely Bradley R. Agle, Thomas Donaldson, R. Edward Freeman, Michael C. Jensen, Ronald K. Mitchell and Donna J. Wood, put their thoughts in the form of essays together and wrote this paper as a kind of dialogue. Their main concern is about the current and future of stakeholder theory in management literature: will the theory in future reflect dynamism, refinement and relevance, or stasis? How will stakeholder theory proceed? Beginning with a review of research and theory that has developed since the major stakeholder theorizing efforts of the 1990s, the authors offer their individual perspectives on the key issues and suggest possible approaches that might advance theory. I will summarize the paper, which includes five contributions.

In the introduction, Agle and Mitchell provide an overview of academic work in the field of stakeholder theory. A table presents existing approaches and studies divided into three areas: normative stakeholder vs. stockholder theory, instrumental stakeholder theory and new questions – further development of stakeholder theory.

In the first contribution, Wood discusses eight assumptions of Chicago School neoclassical economics and concludes that many of them are false. He argues, on the one hand, that free-market policies work wonderfully well for the rich and powerful and that there are many beneficial consequences of the pursuit of self-interest and profit maximization. On the other hand, the author claims that due to the established neoclassical paradigm, life has become much harder for many people and there can be toxic consequences if business's institutional role is ignored (i.e., its relevance and responsibility regarding needs of societies and their people). Wood concludes that, although governments are often inefficient, they are the most effective vehicle for implementing necessary social control mechanisms. Only with such mechanisms in place may societal goals such as human rights and environmental sustainability be achieved. Corporate social responsibility is considered to be the second-best solution in this regard as it is a measure of self-control in conditions of institutional failure to control. However, it bears the opportunity (meant as a disadvantage with respect to societal goals) for companies to make superficial efforts without substance behind them in order to appear good.

In the second contribution, Freeman elaborates on the so-called 'Friedman–Freeman' debate and claims that he ends the debate. He starts by discussing four ideas about how stakeholder theory could get off the ground. (1) In regards to the 'separation thesis', Freeman states that it is not useful to separate questions of business and ethics. (2) Instead, 'the integration thesis' suggests that both should go together and we should build into our normative (i.e., ethical) ideals the need to understand how we create value. (3) In discussion of the 'responsible principle', the author illustrates his belief that most people most of the time want to take responsibility for the results of their actions and, as such, this just supports the integration thesis. (4) In order to go in this direction, Freedman refers to the 'open question argument' stating that for any decision that a manager or other organization member makes, specific questions with respect to the effects and consequences of the action have to be answered. Based on these four ideas, he then claims that there is no real difference between the main arguments of Friedman and himself; only the wording is different. In his view, it is not the purpose of a company to maximize profits; instead, this is the outcome of a well-managed company that requires respecting and taking into account a firm's stakeholders. If there are any conflicts in stakeholder interests or claims, it is the manager's responsibility to rethink the problem and find a solution that creates more value for both. This approach maximizes the profit of the firm.

In the third contribution, Jensen emphasizes the role of the government and values in the stakeholder and profit discussion. On the one hand, he argues that maximizing a firm's profits does not entail maximizing the value of the entire company, notably not producing maximum value for society. Thus, the essential role of government is that citizens give the government the monopoly on the right to set rules and control them. On the other hand, Jensen asks the question, how would we get managers to see that narrow-minded short-term value maximization leads to harm? His answer is that more emphasis has to be put on the role of normative values, how they arise and create conflict and destruction.

In the fourth contribution, Donaldson tells two stories. The first one is about Copernican revolution, which describes the shift from considering the Earth at the center of the universe, towards the heliocentric model with the Sun at the center of the universe. The second one is about the academic discussion regarding the role and evolution of the firm. Starting from Adam Smith the author describes different perspectives and understandings; he ends up with the conclusion that we now enter the stage of a normative revolution. From this revolution two important insights can be drawn: any economic system or institution whatsoever stands in need of normative justification; and managers must ascribe some intrinsic worth to stakeholders.

In the fifth contribution, Mitchell discusses the concept of the joint-stake company, a reference to the term joint-stock company coined by John Stuart Mill. In the center of his debate, Mitchell analyzes the current ('here') and the artificial, joint-stake oriented ('there') way of accounting practices. He argues that a new system-based accounting equation could be comprised of the production and the distribution value. Mitchell challenges the debate by posing several questions and invites research to start thinking in a more 'what-if'-oriented manner.

The conclusion summarizes the debate by emphasizing that questions remain and stakeholder theory still further needs to be built upon. The paper closes with the idea that superior stakeholder theory as suggested by Clarkson (1998) is a dream and could serve as a means for fulfillment. Overall, the paper is very inspiring and a 'must' to read for scholars investigating and refining stakeholder theory. Many aspects covered and discussed help us to understand the roots of stakeholder theory and build new theoretical hypotheses in the realm of the firm's relation with its business environment.

Reference

Clarkson, M.B.E. 1998. Introduction. In M.B.E. Clarkson (ed.), *The Corporation and its Stakeholders – Classic and Contemporary Readings*. Toronto: University of Toronto Press, pp. 1–9.

Bansal, P. and Clelland, I. 2004. Talking trash: Legitimacy, impression management, and unsystematic risk in the context of the natural environment. *Academy of Management Journal*, 47(1): 93–103.

This article takes an institutional theory view to investigate the concepts of environmental legitimacy, impression management with regard to the firm's environmental performance, and corporate financial risk. Many articles have examined how environmental management of a firm's level of emissions has or should have an effect on corporate financial performance. In this article, Bansal and Clelland go beyond this debate and focus on a new aspect of corporate unsystematic risk and efforts to reduce this risk within the context of the natural environment (within the domain of ONE research).

Applying institutional theory, the authors develop four hypotheses. Firms with higher corporate environmental legitimacy will experience lower unsystematic risk (H1). Firms that voluntarily disclose environmental liabilities will experience higher unsystematic risk (H2). The voluntary disclosure of environmental liabilities moderates the relationship between corporate environmental legitimacy and unsystematic risk; this relationship will be stronger for firms that do not disclose environmental liabilities (H3). Expression of environmental commitment moderates the relationship between corporate environmental legitimacy and unsystematic risk; this relationship will be stronger for firms not expressing environmental commitment (H4).

Using a variety of sources and analytical methods with data for the time period 1990–94, the authors come to the following results. Hypothesis 1 is supported and thus, the authors conclude that firms should manage their environmental performance and, in response to that, media will report in a positive way about the firm. This reduces the unsystematic risk of the firm. Support for Hypothesis 2 leads to a conclusion that any new information in the market about a firm's liabilities in the natural environment context increases the firm's unsystematic risk. Hypothesis 3 is not supported and Hypothesis 4 finds moderate support. Bansal and Clelland interpret this result; firms with low environmental legitimacy may reduce their unsystematic risk by expressing commitments to the natural environment. Therefore, firms are somewhat able to manage the perception of their legitimacy. However, the risk of 'green-washing' is evident.

Bansal and Clelland's paper is an important contribution to the ONE literature. Their study addresses corporate risk as an important aspect for scholars and managers outside of the natural environment debate and merges this concept with institutional logics driven by environmental legitimacy. From both theoretical and methodological perspectives, this paper is excellent; it is one of the first papers in which ONE scholars (investigating the relationship between corporate financial performance and environmental/social aspects) analyze non-linear relationships by means of moderation. The research provides direction for the field in the coming years. The authors specifically outline some questions for future research; for example, what is the role of institutions in influencing the long-term unsystematic risk of firms? Especially in light of international climate policy efforts, this would be a very interesting aspect to study.

Hull, C.E. and Rothenberg, S. 2008. Firm performance: The interactions of corporate social performance with innovation and industry differentiation. *Strategic Management Journal*, **29(7): 781–9.**

The question of whether efforts to improve corporate environmental and/or social performance (CSP, note: environmental considerations are included in this term) have an effect on corporate financial performance (CFP) has engaged academics for over 30 years. Results of several meta-analyses are mixed, finding positive, negative and insignificant relationships.

Hull and Rothenberg turn to two articles in the *Strategic Management Journal* to analyze the debate. First, Waddock and Graves (1997) use KLD data in order to investigate the relationship between CSP and CFP; they find a positive relationship. Second, McWilliams and Siegel (2000) argue that Waddock and Graves' analysis is misspecified since the effect of innovation on CFP is neglected. Using the same data, they show that on inclusion of innovation in the analysis, the previously found positive relationship disappears. Hull and Rothenberg base their argument on this finding but argue that the innovation moderates the CSP/CFP relationship. They find support for this hypothesis: their results show that CSP more positively impacts CFP of firms that are low in innovation. Furthermore, the authors investigate whether the level of industry differentiation has a similar moderating effect; CSP does have a higher impact on CFP of firms in industries that have a low level of differentiation.

Hull and Rothenberg reflect on their results and argue that they find support for the initial argument made by Waddock and Graves (1997); CSP indeed pays off. Their interaction result shows that firms with a low level of innovation may use CSP as a strategy to increase profitability. Also, managers in industries having low levels of differentiation (typically commodity industries) may find CSP a valuable asset in the quest for differentiation.

Their study is very interesting and relevant, especially in light of the ongoing CSP/CFP relationship debate. Future studies can refer to Hull and Rothenberg's methodological approach to further investigate the interplay of CSP, innovation, CFP and other relevant factors in this domain. As such, it is an important contribution to this field. In minor ways, the paper is confusing. In the results section on page 785 the authors state that CSP (in Model 2) shows little sign of directly affecting CFP. Instead, Table 2 reports that there is no statistically significant relation at all. Furthermore, the authors state that they find support for Hypotheses 1 and 2 and not for 3. Instead, results show they have support for Hypotheses 2 and 3 and not Hypothesis 1. Beyond this, the paper is excellently written and very relevant for scholars investigating the CSP/CFP relationship.

References

McWilliams, A. and Siegel, D. 2000. Corporate social responsibility and financial performance. Correlation or misspecification? *Strategic Management Journal*, **21**(5), 603–9.
Waddock, S.A. and Graves, S.B. 1997. The corporate social performance–financial performance link. *Strategic Management Journal*, **18**(4), 303–19.

REVIEWS BY TOM COOPER

Matten, D. and Crane, A. 2005. Corporate citizenship: Toward an extended theoretical conceptualization. *Academy of Management Review*, **30(1): 166–79.**

Matten and Crane (2008) critically examine the content of contemporary understandings of corporate citizenship (CC). The concept of CC, which has been widely adopted by practitioners in the corporate social responsibility (CSR) field, is a relatively new development in the business and society literature. Matten and Crane's articles focus on developing a theoretically informed definition of corporate citizenship that is descriptively robust and conceptually distinct from existing concepts in CSR.

Taking the view of citizenship from the academic discipline of political science, the article exposes the misleading use of citizenship terminology in most of the management literature. It also argues that a more precise definition of CC may assist academics and practitioners to understand significant changes in the role of corporations.

First, Matten and Crane outline the origin of CC. Specifically they describe CC emerging from the work of Carroll and his model of corporate responsibilities: economic, legal, ethical and philanthropic. The article provides a good review of the literature around CSR, including stakeholder theory and corporate social performance. The key differentiation in CC is that it emerges from the practitioner rather than the academic literature. Corporate actors use the CC concept in their literature (the article outlines examples of ExxonMobil, Ford, Nokia, etc.). Even so, no clear, specific and widely accepted definition of CC exists.

Second, the authors argue that the current use of the term 'corporate citizenship', otherwise known as corporate philanthropy, can be seen from either the *limited* or *equivalent* view. In the limited view, CC is charitable donations and other forms of community action. Proponents of this limited view tend to argue that the new contribution of CC to the debate on corporate philanthropy is its strategic focus. For example, Matten and Crane give the example of Texas Instruments, whose approach is 'giving back' to communities in which it operates. The strategic reason for this approach is to try to make these communities better places to do business. In the limited approach there is therefore a strategy to focus attention on the direct, physical environment of the company – local communities.

Ultimately the limited approach is merely an extension of (enlightened) self-interest. As the authors indicate, this does not justify the development of a new term such as CC. Moreover, self-interest by business organizations is not usually referred to as 'citizenship', which causes further confusion in the academic and business literature. The limited approach to CC needs to be more than it is to justify academic attention.

The equivalent approach to CC encompasses Carroll's four aspects of CSR – economic, legal, ethical and philanthropic; the article argues that it is a 'rebranding' of CSR with a focus more on 'meeting' obligations. This performance-based perspective of CC reflects the development of the term in the practitioner literature. The authors decide that there is little in the equivalent view of CC that reflects the notion of what is meant by citizenship or its potential for creating new meaning.

Through the use of political theory, the concept of CC is further extended by the authors. Importantly, they note that they take a 'liberal' political stand, which they contend is the principal template for Western democracy. Through an exploration of what is citizenship, Matten and Crane outline the different rights that accrue to individuals. In political theory, individual citizen rights are social, civil and political. The problem with the perspective of CC when citizens are regarded as 'individuals', is that the rights cannot be regarded as an entitlement. The authors use Wood and Logsdon (2001) to argue that although corporations do not have an entitlement to certain individual rights, they remain powerful public actors who have a responsibility in respect of individual citizen's rights.

Instead of addressing the normative elements of corporate responsibility, Matten and Crane opt for a descriptive perspective. They describe the corporate uptake of government functions to render corporate involvement in 'citizenship' a largely unavoidable occurrence. In their belief, this uptake of government functions justifies the shift towards the terminology of CC.

Through the argument that corporate involvement in citizenship is unavoidable, Matten and Crane therefore define CC as describing the role of the corporation in administering citizenship rights for individuals. In the administration of rights they refer to the corporation as a provider, enabler and channel. This moves the CC literature away from the normative context to one of describing what the corporation actually does in respect to citizenship.

As outlined by the authors, the implications of the approach to CC as an administrator of rights are significant. First, moving away from the view of corporations as 'private' citizens means that managers can see the corporation as a provider of specific government functions. Second, the authors' extended conceptualization suggests a replacement label to CC such as 'corporate administration of citizenship', which may confuse the field even more. Third, corporations enter the area of citizenship on a discretionary basis – they are not compelled to administer traditional government responsibilities. However, when they do enter the field, questions emerge from a normative basis as to the level of accountability and scrutiny that they should undertake.

The need for further empirical research about what corporations do in the administration of citizenship rights reveals one of the weaknesses of the paper. It is unclear whether corporations administer rights acting as 'providers, enablers and channels'. The examples that Matten and Crane use to demonstrate the limited view point of corporate citizenship are not focused on administering any particular rights. Although the paper does point to some of the normative elements surrounding CC, it would have been useful to have a more detailed explanation. For example, while it is clear they have covered the enlightened self-interest area of normative theory there are a number of different perspectives that may have assisted in broadening their extended conceptualization. For example, as they indicate, corporations are not compelled to administer citizenship rights. But, from a deontological perspective, what specific duties are they addressing in administering these rights?

Matten and Crane also do not address completely the argument that CC is no different than a practitioner view of social contract theory as exemplified in the work of Donaldson and Dunfee. The authors may also add criticism that CC is just a social contract approach to viewing CSR dressed up in practitioner clothing.

Finally, it is unclear in the article's extended conceptualization of CC, how the corporation differs from any third-party provider of services on behalf of a government. The authors are vague on whether the corporation is taking on the administration of citizenship rights due to an absence of government involvement, better management on behalf of a corporation or, as the article contends, fundamental shifts in business and society relationships. Ultimately, the paper is limited by a liberal political Western viewpoint that eliminates a significant majority of global corporations. As the recent economic crisis has demonstrated, we live in a global world and a descriptive approach to CC cannot be necessarily limited by a liberal, political tradition as the majority of today's global business society did not emerge from or at least understand this tradition. However, the paper provides an excellent addition to the academic debate on the subject of CC and provides many useful avenues for researchers.

Reference

Wood, D.J. and Logsdon, J.M. 2001. Theorising business citizenship. In J. Andriof and M. McIntosh (eds), *Perspectives on Corporate Citizenship*. Sheffield: Greenleaf, pp. 83–103.

Starkey, K. and Crane, A. 2003. Toward green narrative: Management and the evolutionary epic. *Academy of Management Review*, **28(2): 220–37.**

In their article, Starkey and Crane explore the use of narrative to understand the relevance of the sciences in addressing the issue of ecology for management theory and practice. The authors outline the green narrative, specifically the notion of the 'evolutionary epic', to better explain concepts within management theory and practice. The stated aim of the article is to facilitate an understanding of how a newly emergent narrative of nature might challenge mental models regarding the link between management and ecosystem. Ultimately, the authors hope that this green narrative may provide the basis for a shift in management thought on ecology and the environment.

The article discusses the interplay between environment, organization and management. As the authors indicate, the notion of narrative has been well discussed in the management literature, especially those taking a critical perspective. Although narratives' overall impact on management theory is debatable, they contend a broad consensus exists that they can be extremely important in facilitating, shaping and/or preventing change. This 'change' element is vital in the authors' stated purpose of the paper to drive forward a change in thinking surrounding management and the environment.

A narrative approach to management and organization traditionally focuses on sense-making in communication and interpretation of meaning. The contrast is with the logico-scientific approach to thought as outlined by Bruner (1996). Starkey and Crane are not critical and do not choose one approach over another, rather they outline how they are used in the management literature. As the authors argue, a number of competing perspectives have been developed in which scholars seek to provide an alternative to the technocentric understanding of our relationship to nature. This understanding is based on the environment being seen as valuable and inseparable from humanity, which may be better explained through narrative.

As outlined by Tskoukas and Hatch, 2001, narrative can draw our attention to blind spots and help us see what we could not see before: that key concepts do not so much constitute a theory with predictive validity as provide a guide for interpretation. The interpretation that the Starkey and Crane article centers on is the need for better thinking on the nature of the environment and its role in management thinking. The authors contend this may be better explained by narratives rather than searching for scientific certainty.

The authors contend that it is possible to discern significant yet largely unexamined parallels between the shifts stressed by the new environmental paradigm and turns towards a re-enchantment of nature in science. The evolutionary epic can be located at the intersection of these shifts and turns. Taking scientific knowledge about biological evolution into an account of the origin and the evolution of life, the evolutionary epic can therefore provide a defamiliarizing narrative that, while based on the familiar science of evolution, may suggest fundamentally different ways of thinking about management theory and practice.

The concept of the evolutionary epic is introduced within the article as a way of narrating the state of nature. The evolutionary epic is based on the interpretation of an emerging body of scientific literature about the history of life on earth including the seven ages in life's evolution toward greater complexity: chemistry, information, protocell, single cell, multicellular organism, mind and the unknown. Starkey and Crane examine how this theory is consistent with some of the narratives we see in the management literature. The most salient example the authors use is that of Peters and Waterman's *In Search of Excellence* (1982). A problem then emerges in the literature due to the use of management theorists' framing their understanding of the environment within Enlightenment assumptions of a detached and denatured science combined with the belief in technological development and unlimited progress.

Starkey and Crane argue that the evolutionary epic as a narrative may be used to facilitate paradigm shifts in management's thinking towards the environment. One of the key findings of the paper is that there has been extremely scant research on the role of narrative in environmental management. Environmental issues (and indeed narratives) are often perceived as 'soft' aspects of management theory and practice, so the science underpinning the evolutionary epic lends an important aspect of 'hardness' that enhances legitimacy. The authors argue that the evolutionary epic may be seen as an extremely valuable resource for ushering in new understandings and relationships between management and the natural environment.

The primary elements of the evolutionary epic narrative that are especially relevant for management are embedded within the narrative's structure, content and language. This exposes a weakness of the paper. The authors do use some brief examples to explain the content nature of the narrative – such as Brent Spar and product development at Xerox – but the reader is left with a yearning for more elaboration of how the narrative can be used. Language is also explained using such examples as the McDonald's–EDF alliance as well as IKEA's use of the 'Natural Step' program. Once again, this is a very small part of the article and although the arguments that the authors make for using the evolutionary epic as a form of paradigmatic change are strong, readers are left asking how it could be used in practice or in an academic setting. As a strong alternative line of argumentation for changing the view of how management sees the environmental and ecological issue, the paper is excellent and a significant addition to the academic literature.

References

Bruner, J. 1996. The narrative construal of reality. In J. Bruner (ed.), *The Culture of Education*. Cambridge, MA: Harvard University Press, pp. 130–49.
Peters, T.J. and Waterman, R.H. 1982. *In Search of Excellence*. New York: Harper & Row.
Tsoukas, H. and Hatch, M.J. 2001. Complex thinking, complex practice: The case for a narrative approach to organizational complexity. *Human Relations*, **54**(8): 979–1013.

Parker, M. and Pearson, G. 2005. Capitalism and its regulation: A dialogue on business and ethics. *Journal of Business Ethics*, 60(1): 91–101.

The current financial crisis has proved to be an excellent time to be a business school academic. Larger questions of capitalism, regulation and the role of business and society have moved beyond the ivory tower to the mainstream media. When both US and international mainstream news media start to question the role of capitalism in society and whether it is the most appropriate model to drive forward progress, prosperity and equality, who are better placed to weigh in on the subject than the people who get paid to think about these issues – namely business school academics.

Martin Parker and Gordon Pearson foreshadowed the increasing need to examine capitalism and its regulation in their excellent article from 2005 'Capitalism and regulation: A dialogue on business and ethics'. The reader is first of all struck by the format of the article. Echoing the work of the ancient Greeks, the authors have framed the article as a dialogue between two friends with different views. Parker takes the view of the critic of capitalism, while Pearson expounds the virtues of the current capitalistic model. Although the authors contend one is a 'business pragmatist' (Pearson) and the other 'an academic idealist' (Parker), what the reader obtains are some excellent insights as well as use of the academic literature on the fundamental system underlying business and society.

Parker begins with a Marxist view that capitalism has some damaging social consequences. He states that when capitalists make a profit, they are essentially stealing value that is produced by labor; thus, Parker argues that capitalism is a system that maximizes inequalities and encourages an extreme competitive individualism resulting in alienated labor and a damaged sense of community and cooperation. Pearson, on the other hand, believes capitalism is unavoidable and that the Marxist view is based on language that is emotionally charged. The authors are divided on a definition of capitalism and agree that the essential difference is related to the division of labor. The division of labor is a common feature but not an exclusive one in a capitalist system. However, as echoed by Durkheim, the authors contend the division of labor does lead to a sense of alienation. As Pearson indicates, the use of capital in the form of plant and equipment has a far greater impact on productivity in modern day situations that may be seen as a trade-off for the development of alienation. Questions about the ownership of capital are also debated by the authors.

The main part of the paper sees the authors tackle the issue of competition, whereby some succeed and others fail. The capitalist assumption is that pleasing the customer brings success. Parker contends that it is an incorrect assumption since it is based on the premise that because something exists it is what the consumer wants. However, neither author disputes that there is popular suspicion and disquiet about the aggressive market discipline and corporate giganticism that exemplify capitalism.

Finally, the authors have an interesting discourse on regulation. Pearson would like to examine the dominant view that all barriers to trade should be knocked down in order that the 'market' can deliver on its heroic promise of making sure that the supply and demand curves meet in the optimum. Parker contends that the 'market' is not in any sense a level playing field, and is actually dominated by large corporations and the institutions that speak on their behalf. The overall effect of regulation, the article argues, is to make it harder to satisfy customers and generate the wealth that alleviates poverty. Pearson argues for self-regulation, proposing a number of suggestions that might inhibit the greedy and criminal, including limitations on a company's shareholders, corporate governance issues as well as the role of auditors.

Parker wishes that a Socratic dialogue would allow for better examination of prejudices and find common ground. Instead, there is just a reiteration of differences that is one of the article's weaknesses. The article lacks any certainty and its contribution is principally in its approach; also, it foreshadows the current debate on capitalism. The language, especially of Parker, strays too far into rhetoric rather than reasoned, measured argumentation. Ultimately emotion gets the better of the authors but is this necessarily a bad thing – especially when considering the current economic crisis?

Pearson indicates emotion may be laudable, even heroic in the promotion of a non-capitalist society but it does not produce lasting solutions to the sort of problems seen in business and society. Pearson further expounds that capitalism may produce its discontents but heroic utopianism has generally failed to put bread on the table. The article's greatest contribution is in its concluding observation 'We have tried to learn something from each other, but have not come to any precise and accurate answers'. Ultimately, this observation will be applicable to the reinvigorated debate on capitalism as well as its role in business and society. What the reader learns from the article is a new perspective on an old debate – one that potentially does not have any precise or accurate answers but that does produce a significant contribution to the examination of corporate social responsibility.

REVIEWS BY DAINA MAZUTIS

Husted, B.W. and Allen, D.B. 2006. Corporate social responsibility in the multinational enterprise: Strategic and institutional approaches. *Journal of International Business Studies*, **37(6): 838–49.**

Husted and Allen (2006) ask, 'What is the relationship of global and local (country-specific) corporate social responsibility (CSR) to international organizational strategy?' This is an underexamined area in both CSR and international business research and, although empirical, the paper's primary contribution is to theory. It is one of the first and only papers to make the distinction between local and global CSR issues. Most empirical work on CSR takes a composite measure of CSP (e.g., KLD data) that includes a wide range of CSR issues. Husted and Allen (2006) distinguish between 'local CSR' that reflects a firm's responsibilities to its local community vs. 'global CSR' that reflects a firm's responsibilities based on universal hypernorms or 'standards to which all societies can be held'. Although the methodology used to test for this distinction is problematic, this more fine-grained articulation of CSR is a contribution to theory in the field.

After discussing the difference between local and global CSR, the authors set up competing hypotheses to examine how different MNE strategies (multidomestic, transnational or global) respond to local vs. global CSR issues. They first argue that it is possible that MNEs align their CSR strategies similarly to how they select a local or global product/market strategy based on the need for integration or responsiveness (this is mirrored in Bartlett and Ghoshal's, 1989 typology). They call this the strategic approach. Alternatively, MNEs might simply be reacting to isomorphic pressures within the firm when setting up organizational strategies – or, in other words, following the institutional approach.

Data was collected through a survey sent to CEOs in Mexico (final n = 111). The dependent variable is type of organizational strategy – multidomestic, transnational or global – which was measured through four-scale items (economies of scale, global competition, domestic competition and national responsiveness). The independent variables (local vs. global CSR) were measured by single-scale items on the importance of job creation (local CSR) and the environment (global CSR) on the business mission. Two other more ambiguous CSR issues (support of social causes and collaboration in community projects) were also measured. Cluster analysis was used to first segment the firms into multidomestic, transnational or global firms. Then, discriminant analysis and multinomial logit were used to test the hypotheses.

The authors found that job creation (or local CSR) is the best indicator for type of organizational strategy; the environment was not a predictor of type of MNE. These results held after controlling for size, industry sector and country of origin. Specifically, local CSR (job creation) is more common among multidomestic and transnational MNEs than among global MNEs. Global CSR (as measured by importance of the environment) is equally common among all types of MNEs. The authors claim that their findings support the institutional approach to CSR as 'CSR seems to conform to the MNE organization strategy established for product-market activities' (p. 846).

Although the primary contribution of this paper lies with the distinction of local vs. global CSR, the operationalization of these constructs is somewhat problematic. The study includes just a single-scale item on the importance of job creation as the operationalization of local CSR. Similarly, global CSR is measured as the importance of the environment to the business mission. This does not seem to adequately capture the scope of this important theoretical distinction.

Theoretically, the 'strategic vs. institutional' approaches to organizational strategy could also have been better articulated. The rationale based on Bartlett and Ghoshal (1989) that leads up to the first hypothesis seems to indicate the opposite of what is actually hypothesized. Furthermore, the second set of institutional arguments is not very well grounded in institutional theory. For example, the 'isomorphic pressures' described here occur within the firm (e.g., the CSR department is modeled after the marketing department), whereas traditionally, 'isomorphic pressures' are used to describe why so many firms within an industry or field are so similar. Although the authors claim to have made a theoretical contribution to the 'usefulness of institutional theory in explaining the adoption of CSR policies' (p. 847), this is not entirely convincing.

The paper's primary problems, however, are methodological. Given that a single survey design was used to collect data on both the independent and dependent variables, common method bias concerns should have been addressed. Furthermore, no information is provided on the reliability or internal consistency of the scale items, and there appears to be only a single item to measure each of the CSR issues. This raises further questions of construct validity. Both the inference and direction of causality are also confounded in the presentation of results.

Despite these theoretical and methodological issues, this study provides a starting point for the discussion of different types of CSR (local vs. global) and how these relate to different MNE strategies. In this regard, the article offers an important contribution to both the CSR and international business fields.

Reference

Bartlett, C.A. and Ghoshal, S. 1989. *Managing Across Borders: The Transnational Solution.* Boston, MA: Harvard University Press.

Rose, J.M. 2007. Corporate directors and social responsibility: Ethics versus shareholder value. *Journal of Business Ethics*, **73(3): 319–31.**

In 'Corporate directors and social responsibility' (2007), Rose explores the question of how directors go about making decisions regarding social and ethical dilemmas. This study presents the results of an experiment conducted with active directors of US Fortune 200 companies. Although the sample is small, Rose is one of very few researchers who has gained primary access to Board of Director members and directly tested decision-making in regards to CSR and ethical dilemmas. Follow-up interviews add reliability and validity to the study's disturbing findings that 'corporate leaders make decisions that emphasize legal defensibility, rather than ethics or social responsibility' (p. 320).

Work in business ethics and social responsibility tends to blame ethical crises either on the lack of personal moral standards of business leaders and/or business education's lack of focus on ethical training. Less attention, however, has been given to the role that the legal environment plays in managerial decision-making. The author claims that ethical decision-making must take this critical aspect into consideration as directors are legally required to first maximize shareholder value. Thus, when facing an ethical dilemma, through the mechanism of prospective rationality (knowing that their decisions will have to be justified in the future), directors will choose strategies that are more legally defensible rather than what is 'better for society'.

Rose uses an experimental design (2×2) with 34 active directors of US Fortune 200 firms. The experiment consists of reading two cases and answering questions. The first case presents a dilemma regarding the cutting of old-growth forests (this had environmental and social considerations, but no threat to human health). The second scenario presents a case where the board has to decide whether or not to invest in new technologies to reduce toxic emissions (this has environmental, social and human health implications). The independent variable, 'duty to shareholders', was manipulated by changing the decision perspective (either director or partner in private firm) for half the participants. The second independent variable, 'social threat level', was manipulated through the cases with the first having no threat to human health and safety. The dependent variable was the participants' actual decision (cut/not cut forest; invest/not invest in technology to limit toxic emission).

The author also administered a follow-up questionnaire and conducted debriefing interviews.

In summarizing his findings, Rose states: 'When directors made decisions from the perspective of a corporate director, all but one director chose to cut the old-growth forest and all but two directors voted to continue to emit [the cancerous toxin]' (p. 325). This was statistically different for those participants acting from the perspective of a partner in a private firm where 41 percent voted against cutting the forest and 82 percent voted to reduce emissions. Participants acting as partners were also more sensitive to the case with the higher level of social threat.

During follow-up one-on-one interviews, every participant recognized the ethical dilemma and the implied trade-offs, suggesting that further ethics education is not the answer. The participants acting as directors explained that their primary duty is to the shareholder and that they were legally required to cut the forest/continue to emit the toxin to maximize shareholder value. Directors employ a hierarchy of decision-criteria, which starts with obeying the law, meeting duties to shareholders and then making legally defensible decisions to protect personal liability (p. 328). If making the socially responsible decision violates any of these criteria, despite recognizing the ethical dilemma, directors will intentionally harm society. When free of these duties (as in the partner case), participants were more willing to make the non-profit-maximizing decisions and help the environment or society. The outlier in the director experiment, who would not cut the old-growth forest, was a Social Responsibility Officer on several boards.

This article is very well written, the theory is compelling, the methodology is sound and the findings are interesting. Although the sample is very small, and the decisions arguably simplistic, it is still shocking to learn that legal considerations will trump ethical or social considerations in both cases that harm the environment and harm other humans. This is counter-intuitive given that the author presents the results of previous studies that indicate that corporate directors and executive leaders have higher levels of moral reasoning than their peers. The implication is that they suppress their ethical compass in order to be perceived as independent and objective, a condition that is imposed upon directors through legal frameworks such as Sarbanes–Oxley. It is also sobering to think that more ethical training in business schools or executive development programs will not influence these results; only changes in external legal frameworks or the composition of boards (to include Social Responsibility Officers) may lead to more ethical decisions. The latter, at least, should be a promising avenue for future research.

Hillman, A.J. and Keim, G.D. 2001. Shareholder value, stakeholder management, and social issues: What's the bottom line? *Strategic Management Journal*, **22(2): 125–39.**

Hillman and Keim (2001) seek to answer the oft-asked question: 'When firms engage in social issues unrelated to obligations to direct stakeholders, what is the effect on firm performance?' One of the main contributions of this research is its more fine-grained distinction between stakeholder management and social issue participation. The former includes a firm's relationships with actors who have a direct influence on the success of the firm (employees, suppliers, customers etc.). The latter, social issue participation, refers to firms that engage in industries and activities that are perceived to have an ethical component (e.g., tobacco/firearms industries or investment in countries with human rights abuses). Despite this important theoretical distinction and the interesting empirical findings, the operationalization of the constructs is somewhat problematic.

Using stakeholder theory and RBV, more specifically the VRIO (Value, Rarity, Imitability, Organization) nature of positive stakeholder relationships, the authors posit that stakeholder management will lead to improved shareholder value creation. By the same logic, choosing to engage in social issues may not lead to improved firm performance as the benefits accrued to the firm are likely not to be valuable, rare or inimitable.

In their study, 'shareholder value creation' is operationalized as MVA (market value-added); 'stakeholder management' is measured using five categories from KLD: employee relations, diversity issues, product issues, community relations and environmental issues. Social issue participation (SIP) is measured using the KLD categories of 'other/alcohol/tobacco/gambling', 'military', 'nuclear power', 'non-US' and 'concerns over investment in Burma and Mexico' screens. Controls include size, industry and risk. Correlation analysis and regression were used to test the hypotheses on a sample of 308 firms.

The authors find that stakeholder management and shareholder value are significantly correlated and, when regressed, stakeholder management is positively and significantly associated with improved shareholder value. In contrast, social issue participation is significantly and negatively correlated with shareholder value. Again, when regressed, social issue performance has a negative impact on shareholder value creation. In post-hoc analyses, reverse causality was not supported.

As with other studies using KLD data, some theoretical issues arise as they pertain to the measurement of the dependent variable. Here, the authors have chosen not to assign any weights to the various categories, but rather to use a simple sum of strengths and weaknesses. Since the publication of this article, others have shown that this is not an ideal manner in which to capture CSR as firms can be both 'very responsible' in some categories and 'very irresponsible' in others, effectively canceling out the effect of either (Strike et al., 2006). Furthermore, the authors do not include other control variables, such as past financial performance and R&D expenditure, which have been shown to impact CSP.

The authors conclude by stating that their 'findings suggest that if the activity is directly tied to primary stakeholders, then investments may benefit not only stakeholders but also result in increased shareholder wealth. Participating in social issues beyond the direct stakeholders, however, may adversely affect a firm's ability to create shareholder wealth (p. 135)'. The operationalization of social issues is primarily the KLD screen for firms whose primary industry is either alcohol, tobacco, firearms, nuclear or military. This means that the dependent variable is more or less binary and that those firms in these select 'socially-debatable' industries have created less shareholder returns than firms in other industries overall. It is not really a measure of 'regular' firms investing in social issues – construct validity, then, also becomes a question. This also suggests that the primary research question, 'When firms engage in social issues unrelated to obligations to direct stakeholders, what is the effect on firm performance?' cannot be answered with this methodology as the two sets of firms are separated.

The theoretical distinction, however, is still important and warrants further analysis. Many of the KLD category items that are used to measure stakeholder management might be better reassigned to measure 'social-issue participation'. For example, the community relations category includes a measure for 'prominent participation in public/private initiatives that support housing initiatives for the economically disadvantaged'. This seems to be a better indicator of social issue participation than stakeholder management if the definition adopted by the authors is used. Thus, although the more fine-grained distinction of CSR posited in this article is a theoretical contribution, methodologically, this distinction can still be developed.

Reference

Strike, V.M., Gao, J. and Bansal, P. 2006. Being good while being bad: Social responsibility and the international diversification of US firms. *Journal of International Business Studies*, **37**(6): 850.

REVIEWS BY JOSEPHINE STOMP

Maguire, S. and Hardy, C. 2006. The emergence of new global institutions: A discursive perspective. *Organization Studies*, **27(1): 7–29.**

From the perspective of institutional theory, Maguire and Hardy explore the role of discourse and actors at a global level of analysis in the shift from environmental regulatory framework based on empirical evidence of harm to the adoption of a framework based on potential for harm in the face of lack of empirical evidence. They dub the former approach 'sound science' and the latter as 'precautionary science'. The case that Maguire and Hardy explore is the 2004 Stockholm Convention on Persistent Organic Pollutants (POPs); POPs include chemical compounds known as the 'dirty dozen' and include DDT and PCBs.

The 2004 Stockholm Convention eliminated or restricted the use of these compounds and provided a process for the elimination or restriction of other potentially dangerous compounds based on the potential for harm rather than evidence of harm. The Convention presents a significant tipping point in the delegitimization of sound science that privileges corporate actors with considerable financial resources and motivation to do research that is favorable to their interests and to neglect research that is not. It legitimizes the need for precaution that empowers governments and special interests to resist profit-motivated corporations and create institutions that protect the environment broadly.

The article builds on a prior theoretical contribution by Phillips et al. (2004) on how institutional change is fostered by discursive struggles between actors representing different institutional logics, where discursive struggles are a manifestation of shifts in power between actors. Here the key actors are governments, in particular EU members supported by Norway and Ireland as proponents of precaution, and Japan, the US, Canada, Australia and New Zealand (JUSCANZ countries) as advocates for limits on the scope of precaution; the International POPs Elimination Network, representing 350 NGOs; and the International Council of Chemical Associations representing producers of POPs.

Maguire and Hardy focus on the role of discourse in shaping extant or new institutions. Discourse on issues, however, takes place within a broad cultural framework (see Friedland and Alford, 1991). From this perspective, the Stockholm Convention on POPs is part of a larger challenge to the fallibility and risks of scientific certainty and the delegitimization of science in support of corporate interests juxtaposed against the rising legitimacy of social and ecological concerns and NGOs. Unfortunately, Maguire and Hardy fail to explore the antecedent conditions that led up to the Stockholm Convention and created the seedbed that made adoption of precaution possible and raised non-economic interests over economic interests. In short, new discourses do not, as Maguire and Hardy conclude, lead to new institutions but are a consequence of shifts in societal logics that over time spawn awareness of misalignment of interests, discourse and action (see Seo and Creed, 2002).

In summary, Maguire and Hardy provide a fascinating study of change from evidence-based regulation to precaution-based regulation. It is, however, a partial picture both in relation to power and behavior as a result of their focus on discourse. Institutional theory contributes that cultural, spatial and temporal dimensions add richness to the links between discourse, actors and power in deinstitutionalization and institutionalization processes. Qualitative research, such as case analysis, provides the framework to explore these dimensions. It is unfortunate that Maguire and Hardy did not include this approach.

References

Friedland, R. and Alford, R.R. 1991. Bringing society back in: Symbols, practices and institutional contradictions. In W.W. Powell and P.J. DiMaggio (eds), *The New Institutionalism in Organizational Analysis*. Chicago: The University of Chicago Press, pp. 232–63.
Phillips, N., Lawrence, T.B. and Hardy, C. 2004. Discourse and institutions. *Academy of Management Review*, 29(4), 635–52.
Seo, M. and Creed, W.E.D. 2002. Institutional contradictions, praxis and institutional change: A dialectical perspective. *Academy of Management Review*, 27(2): 222–47.

Maguire, S. and Hardy, C. 2009. Discourse and deinstitutionalization: The decline of DDT. *Academy of Management Journal*, **52(1): 148–78.**

In this 2009 article, Maguire and Hardy focus on the role of Rachel Carson as an exogenous 'institutional entrepreneur' in the 'translation' of DDT from life-saving to life-threatening in the face of 'defensive institutional work' by the producers and proponents of DDT. As in the prior article, the authors link discursive struggles to power struggles. Importantly here, the authors link their findings to Scott's three pillars of institutionalization (2001, 2008) and thus establish a strong foundation for the usefulness of institutional theory in the examination of 'green' issues.

In particular, Maguire and Hardy establish that Carson's (1962) *Silent Spring* shifted scientific discourse and research from the efficacy of DDT as an insecticide to its dangers for birds, fish and mammals and how this spawned research that supported and legitimized Carson's criticism of DDT's safety, albeit it also spawned counter-claims by corporate-sponsored researchers that focused on the relative benefits of DDT. The clash between entrepreneurs and defenders of the status quo explains why DDT was banned by the US Environmental Protection Agency in 1962 on the basis that it was hazardous but the ecological impact of DDT was long regarded as less harmful than the social costs of malaria in Africa.

In turn, Maguire and Hardy compare Carson's *Silent Spring* to Gore's *An Inconvenient Truth* (2006) in regard to the creation of awareness and discussion but point to little indication of changes in consumption or regulation. While they suggest that the UN Intergovernmental Panel on Climate Change may, as result of its Nobel stature, make a difference, a *NY Times* article, 'Nobel halo fades fast for climate change' (4 August 2009), suggests that we need other case studies to explore what conditions promote deinstitutionalization and institutionalization and why some 'green' issues are fads or fashions. Based on the delegitimization of DDT, Maguire and Hardy suggest that is because actors need both to highlight issues and to provide do-able 'green' alternatives. I would recommend that future research looks into this very interesting issue.

I was also struck by Maguire and Hardy's pronouncement that text producers are unable to control how actors translate texts. Yet, whether it is in the realm of news (e.g., Fox), reality television (e.g., *The Bachelorette*), photography (e.g., Photoshop.com) or supposedly neutral websites (e.g., Trip Advisor.com), manipulation in order to control translation occurs widely. Perhaps, researchers need to study the (dis)similarities between big corporations' or vested interests' entrepreneurial actions and individuals', such as Carson and Gore, or NGOs' challenges to giant industries. Based on observation rather than research, it would appear to be that NGOs are becoming increasingly savvy institutional entrepreneurs and manipulators, that is, translators.

In summary, I have highlighted potential gaps but this article makes many strong contributions and in contrast to Maguire and Hardy (2006), is well based in institutional theory. Nonetheless, I urge that the roles of power and context be accounted for to explain persistence, resistance and change and behaviors such as ceremonial compliance.

References

Carson, R. 1962. *Slient Spring*. Boston: Houghton Mifflin.
Gore, A. 2006. *An Inconvenient Truth*. Documentary film directed by David Guggenheim.
Scott, W.R. 2001. *Institutions and Organizations* (2nd edn). Thousand Oaks: Sage.
Scott, W.R. 2008. *Institutions and Organizations: Ideas and Interests* (3rd edn). Thousand Oaks: Sage.

Berrone, P. and Gomez-Meija, L.R. 2009. Environmental performance and executive compensation: An integrated agency–institutional perspective. *Academy of Management Journal*, **52**(1): 103–26.

Berrone and Gomez-Meija (2009) find that CEOs in polluting industries who focus on improvement of their firm's environmental performance are financially rewarded. Their study supports the proposition that institutional theory moderates the principal–agent relationship; in short, CEOs seek to reduce externalities when they are rewarded for environmental citizenship behavior. In turn, Berrone and Gomez-Meija show the robustness of agency theory in regard to accommodation of shareholder and stakeholder interests.

Not perhaps surprising from the perspective of institutional theory (Meyer and Rowan, 1977), Berrone and Gomez-Meija find that a ceremonial interest in green has little impact on CEO behavior. This is likely due to their focus: namely, 'green' as pollution prevention or 'green' as end-of-the-pipe clean-up versus 'green' as impression management. This provides an opportunity for important follow-up in regard to the drivers of behaviors as a continuum ranging from inaction on green issues, adoption of impression management or ceremonial compliance, end-of-pipe clean-up initiatives and pollution prevention strategies (Oliver, 1991).

In turn, the authors note that their study does not look at CEO/firm behavior from the standpoint of variations in regulation across different states or the role of CEOs and/or Board of Directors in rewarding environmental performance. However, states have different regulations. In turn, differences between Jack Walsh and Jeff Immelt at General Electric suggest that CEOs and/or boards impact CEO compensation. In turn, the study opens up the opportunity to investigate the link between HR practices, environmental performance, competitive advantage, legitimacy and financial performance at an organizational level of analysis.

In short, Berrone and Gomez-Meija have made an interesting contribution that links green behaviors to not only key theories – institutional theory and agency theory – but also to key topics – incentives and CEOs' behaviors. It is through these types of research linkages that 'green' issues can, as Maguire and Hardy (2009) have established, make a difference.

References

Meyer, J. and Rowan, B. 1977. Institutional organizations: Formal structure as myth and ceremony. *American Journal of Sociology*, **83**(2): 340–63.
Oliver, C. 1991. Strategic responses to institutional processes. *Academy of Management Review*, **16**(1): 145–79.

4   NGOs, IGOs, government and sustainability in developing nations*
C. Gopinath, Mai Skott Linneberg, Natalie Slawinski and Susan L. Young

OVERVIEW BY NATALIE SLAWINSKI

In the wake of globalization, non-governmental organizations (NGOs), intergovernmental organizations (IGOs), such as the United Nations and World Bank, and government are having an increasing impact on corporations. Recently, this trend has been reflected in the growing research on NGOs in the international management literature (Teegan et al., 2004). Researchers have begun to take a deeper dive into the strategies and culture of NGOs and activists, examining their differences (Lewis, 2003; Den Hond and de Bakker, 2007) and their impacts on multinational corporations (Teegan et al., 2004; Oetzel and Doh, 2009). Despite the increased attention to NGOs, however, the role of IGOs and government has been somewhat absent from management literature. Instead, the study of the impact of IGOs and government on business and local economies has remained the purview of the political science and development literatures (Park, 2007; Firsova and Taplin, 2009). This is unfortunate given that the intersection of research on the public and third sectors with the management literature shows much promise for advancing our understanding of sustainability and international business.

Currently, the study of NGOs, IGOs, government and sustainability in developing nations is fragmented. This is likely due to its interdisciplinary nature. To bring this disparate research closer together, researchers need to clearly articulate definitions of terms such as sustainability, which may have different meanings according to different disciplines. Some researchers appear to take for granted that readers agree upon a definition of sustainability, and as a result do not present one in their work (e.g., Lewis, 2003).

Another gap that remains is that of bridging the different levels of analysis used in research on firms versus research on government, IGOs and

---

* Facilitator: Deborah E. de Lange.

NGOs. One of the likely obstacles to bridging the levels of analysis is the existing theories used in the management literature. Theories such as the resource-based view and stakeholder theory dominate research on sustainability and are at the firm level of analysis (e.g., Sharma and Vredenburg, 1998). Institutional theory shows promise for bridging the field, as does multilevel theorizing (Starik and Rands, 1995), but researchers have yet to use these theoretical frameworks to study the intersection of NGOs, IGOs, government and sustainability in developing nations.

The international management literature also presents gaps that prevent the bridging of the field. For example, two theories of international business and economics, the spillovers perspective and the liability of foreignness (LOF) perspective, have the MNE as their unit of analysis. The spillovers perspective argues that MNEs contribute to the countries in which they operate through spillover effects (benefits that naturally accrue to local firms), and the LOF perspective argues that MNEs must overcome constraints in order to succeed in developing country markets. Neither view has paid much attention to developing countries, focusing attention instead on Triad countries (the US, Western Europe and Japan). And whatever attention has been given to developing countries has focused on the benefits to the MNE rather than to the developing country (Oetzel and Doh, 2009).

Because neither view gives a complete perspective on how MNEs and local economies can both benefit from foreign investment, Oetzel and Doh (2009) offer a third perspective – a resource complementarity perspective – in which MNEs and local NGOs collaborate to allow for social and economic development. This paper fills an important gap of highlighting the increasingly salient role played by local NGOs in MNE investments in developing countries. It therefore attempts to bridge the gap between the international management literature and the development literature.

Other gaps are evident as well, especially regarding the role of government policy. For example, we lack an understanding of how environmental and social policies impact corporate behavior. We also know little about how firms impact IGOs and government. Again, the focus of management literature on the firm as the unit of analysis has focused attention on how firms are impacted rather than on how developing country policy and economics are impacted. We need to ask questions such as, how can multinationals have a positive impact, both environmentally and socially, on the countries in which they operate?

The study of the role of the private sector, public sector and third sector in building sustainability in developing countries is important and ripe for future researchers. More attention should be given to the nature and role of NGOs, IGOs and government. Drawing on other management theories (e.g., social network theory) or developing new theories such as Oetzel and Doh (2009) have done show promise for advancing the field. Finally, management researchers would benefit from drawing on the literature in other disciplinary areas (such as the development and political economy literatures) and incorporating them into current management thinking. In short, the field of green international management is in need of creativity and rigor. This will allow for a much-needed understanding of the complex problem of sustainability in developing countries and the role of multiple sectors.

References

Den Hond, F. and De Bakker, F.G.A. 2007. Ideologically motivated activism: How activist groups influence corporate social change activities. *Academy of Management Review*, **32**(3): 901–24.

Firsova, A. and Taplin, R. 2009. Australia and Russia: How do their environmental policy processes differ? *Environment, Development, and Sustainability*, **11**(2): 407–26.

Lewis, D. 2003. NGOs, organizational culture, and institutional sustainability. *Annals of the American Academy of Political and Social Science*, **590**(1): 212–26.

Oetzel, J. and Doh, J.P. 2009. MNEs and development: A review and reconceptualization. *Journal of World Business*, **44**(2): 108–20.

Park, S. 2007. The World Bank Group: Championing sustainable development norms? *Global Governance*, **13**(4): 535–56.

Sharma, S. and Vredenburg, H. 1998. Proactive corporate environmental strategy and the development of competitively valuable organizational capabilities. *Strategic Management Journal*, **19**(8): 729–53.

Starik, M. and Rands, G.P. 1995. Weaving an integrated web: Multilevel and multisystem perspectives of ecologically sustainable organizations. *Academy of Management Review*, **20**(4): 908–35.

Teegan, H., Doh, J.P. and Vachani, S. 2004. The importance of nongovernmental organizations (NGOs) in global governance and value creation: An international business research agenda. *Journal of International Business Studies*, **35**(6): 463–83.

REVIEWS BY C. GOPINATH

Sharma, S. and Vredenburg, H. 1998. Proactive corporate environmental strategy and the development of competitively valuable organizational capabilities. *Strategic Management Journal*, **19(8): 729–53.**

This paper focuses on the effects of organizational environmental strategies on the same organization's capabilities, and how in turn it affects its competitiveness.

This is an empirical paper and the study was conducted in two phases. The first phase was an exploratory study involving interviews of executives in various companies in the Canadian oil and gas industry. The second phase made use of constructs developed in the first phase to do a mail survey of executives in those companies. The environmental strategies followed are examined along 11 dimensions, and a regression framework is used to test the hypotheses.

The paper uses the resource-based view of the firm as its theoretical framework to argue that there is a two-way relationship between organizational capabilities and competitive strategies. That is, not only do the capabilities of a firm determine the strategies adopted, but certain strategies followed in turn help the firm build capabilities.

The main conclusions of the paper are that proactive environmental strategies helped to develop unique organizational capabilities in the industry. The environmental responsiveness strategies explained about 20 percent of the emergence of organizational capabilities. These capabilities include technological innovations, efforts to reduce waste, reduce energy use and build partnerships and so on.

The paper relies on self-reported (perceptual) measures of organizational capability, and benefits, amongst others, which is an important weakness in the study. The exploratory part of the paper involves in-depth interviews. The authors could have used this data for more than developing constructs, to provide a 'richer' analysis of the variables under study. Perhaps their search for 'rigor' led them to use the regression model. Also, although the authors cite work from the field of organizational learning, they do not use those theories to inform the hypotheses. The paper may have benefited from the use of the organizational learning perspective since they are studying how the organization built its capabilities from the implementation of its strategies.

The oil and gas industry is one that has been under regulatory scrutiny and pressure from environmental groups for many years. Thus, one might expect this industry to be more 'savvy' in how it crafts its environmental strategies. Thus, the generalizability of the conclusions of this study is limited. One important contribution of the paper is the questionnaire survey they have developed to measure environmental strategies.

Sreekumar, T.T. and Parayil, G. 2002. Contentions and contradictions of tourism as development option: The case of Kerala, India. *Third World Quarterly*, **23(3): 529–48.**

The focus of the paper is to evaluate the contribution of tourism to economic development, especially eco-tourism. Tourism is often touted as a sector that can be 'exploited' to serve as an engine of economic growth with minimum negative impact on the environment. The growth of eco-parks around the world is a testimony to this. Thus, this paper examines this issue in a specific context.

The state of Kerala, on the west coast of India, is used as a case study. Kerala is often cited as an example of successful promotion of tourism within the country. The analysis in the paper rests on critical examination of secondary data and there is no use of any statistical techniques. The authors have examined published data sourced from the 'Economic Review' of the state government. They argue that the data show a lack of internal consistency and that the basis on which data are reported is at variance with national statistics. This leads them to challenge the conclusions about the sector arrived at by the state government. They also argue that there are wide variations in the data reported, which leads to doubts about the reliability of the data. Although the authors mention 'unstructured interviews' as data sources, they do not systematically analyze or report the interviews.

The paper relies on theories of economic development and the role of different sectors in contributing to it to provide the theory basis for the arguments. They also cite literature pertaining to 'sustainable tourism' as comprising the interconnected dimensions of ecology, economy and society, and suggest a multidisciplinary perspective as the basis on which this sector needs to be examined.

The main conclusions they arrive at are that tourism remains an inconsequential segment of Kerala's economy even after ten years of governmental backing. This is counter to the state government's projection of tourism as being of great significance for the state.

The state provides subsidies for the promotion of tourism, and thus there is a nexus of bureaucracy and private entrepreneurs to justify the continued preferences and to portray that tourism is a major activity and is successful. However, the authors argue that tourism projects have major environmental implications and need more scrutiny; coastal environmental regulations have been violated on the grounds that tourism is a preferable activity.

While the authors charge a 'conspiracy' at the state level to justify the importance of tourism, they do not provide evidence to support it. Thus, the conclusions that they reach seem to extend beyond their data and analysis. Moreover, while the dimensions of ecology and society are referred to, they are not part of the analytical framework used.

Since their argument rests on challenging the importance attributed to tourism in the state, the data they use, namely earnings generated by the industry, are too narrow on which to base their conclusions. Their arguments could have been strengthened if they had also examined data on employment generated by tourism, secondary and tertiary businesses created, and so forth, to measure the economic impact of the sector.

The paper focuses on an important issue, namely, tourism as a sector that has the potential to alleviate the exploitation of natural resources; it is a critical issue in several developing economies. The paper highlights the political–business–ecological connections of the issue and the need for a multidimensional perspective while examining the issues.

Rudra, N. 2002. Globalization and the decline of the welfare state in less-developed countries. *International Organization*, 56(2): 411–45.

The paper examines the coexistence of globalization with the welfare state. The author proposes a model to examine the determinants of a welfare state and how it affects rich and poor countries differently.

The study examined 53 less developed countries (LDCs) between 1972 and 1995 using cross-sectional time series methods. Capital flows, trade and welfare spending between LDCs and developed countries are compared. The analysis uses econometric models (such as panel regressions), where social security and welfare expenditure are dependent variables, and economic globalization (trade and capital flows) and labor power are independent variables.

The author's argument relies on two theoretical streams. She uses theories from political science that place the role of labor as critical in the outcomes of welfare states, and focuses on labor's contribution to economic development. Referred to as power-resource theories, she argues that the success of a welfare state depends on a well-organized labor movement. The other stream is the economic argument, especially the Stolper–Samuelson theorem, which implies that the most abundant factors of production will gain from openness of the economy.

The author concludes that in the face of globalization, labor in developing countries has not been able to prevent the dismantling of the welfare state, as against their counterparts in the developed countries. Welfare spending in LDCs adjusts according to the level of trade flows and capital mobility and low-skilled workers in these countries are less able to organize against the tide of decreasing welfare.

The author relies on social security spending to judge a welfare state. This may be appropriate for developed countries, but appears a very narrow base for developing countries. To make a convincing argument, the data need to also include other measures such as health and education.

The study has been circumscribed by availability of data, which has limited the sample. This is not unusual, but the exclusion of China and Eastern European countries makes it difficult to accept the conclusions as a generalized statement about developing countries.

Due to their level of economic development, developing countries are constrained in their ability to spend on welfare. Organized labor in these countries uses its power to secure benefits from employers rather than the government; this may explain why labor does not fight to increase welfare spending. The author does not consider this argument. Moreover, studies have argued that IMF conditionalities have also constrained the spending of poorer countries on welfare measures.

Large pools of low-skilled labor that is in surplus in the country tends to offset labor's potential gains from globalization. The author introduces a new concept of potential labor power, by weighting the existence of skilled/low-skilled labor with the percentage of surplus labor in the population, which is an interesting contribution.

REVIEWS BY MAI SKOTT LINNEBERG

Dowell, G., Hart, S. and Yeung Do, B. 2000. Do corporate global environmental standards create or destroy market value? *Management Science*, **46(8): 1059–74.**

The research question of the article, 'Is firm value linked to an MNE's corporate environmental policy?', is timely and relevant both in practice and theory. In practice, MNCs are faced by the challenges of having to implement strategies across diverse subsidiaries and markets. At the same time, they are increasingly regarded as one global corporation and not as a set of national organizations that can act differently in different markets. Moreover, the motive of internationalization as a means to exploit Second and Third World countries is regarded unsustainable and 'inappropriate'.

The position the article takes is to look into whether a single stringent corporate environmental policy has a positive effect on firm value compared with many less stringent policies that are poorly enforced. Arguments are made on both sides of the question of whether a stringent global corporate environmental standard represents a competitive asset or a liability for multinational enterprises investing in emerging and developing markets. The article is positioned within the stream of literature that addresses how environmental performance affects financial performance. The article states that this is a growing body of convergent literature (p. 1061). The article reveals that existing literature is primarily empirical and focuses on MNCs in the US and Europe; there appear to be few conceptual or qualitative research contributions. This article is also empirical and the authors fill a gap in the mentioned literature by examining MNCs that have operations in developing countries.

Through analysis of the effects of global environmental standards on a number of US-based MNEs in relation to their stock market performance, the article finds that firms adopting a single stringent global environmental standard have much higher market values (measured by Tobin's q), than firms adopting less stringent/poorly enforced host country standards. Inverse causal directionality is not dealt with; the article should address the issue that firms with higher market values have more resources to deal with stringent standards than other firms. The results suggest that developing countries offering lax environmental regulations to attract foreign direct investment may end up attracting firms of poorer quality than are desired. In this way, the article addresses a relevant gap in the literature. We conceptually view MNCs as benefitting from their presence in diverse markets so as to draw on the particular attributes of those markets, be they low salaries and sometimes lax regulations. This article is one of the first using this type of empirical data and should spawn additional studies, perhaps some that are qualitative. Future contributions can check and challenge the results of this article to shed light on what happens in developing countries when standards that are formulated by Western MNCs are implemented in these countries. How are they translated? And do they make sense in a different reality?

Jennings, P.D. and Zandbergen, P.A. 1995. Ecologically sustainable organizations: An institutional approach. *The Academy of Management Review*, **20(4): 1015–52.**

The main objective of the article, to show the value of applying an institutional (organizational) theoretical approach to ecologically sustainable organizations, appears rather broad, that is, to investigate if institutional theory may help us to define sustainability and to examine how sustainable practices are generated and adopted. This implies that the authors are extending institutional theory to a new area of study. Accordingly, some of the assumptions of institutional theory are re-examined. Following this, the authors suggest possible modifications to organizational institutional theory.

The article is positioned at the intersection of organization theory and ecology literature: two streams of literature that have overlapping, but different perspectives on sustainability and the respective organizational contributions.

The starting point is institutional theory. It conceptualizes the understanding of how consensus is built around the meaning of sustainability and how concepts or practices associated with sustainability are developed and diffused. The article aims to extend institutional theory and hence offers a series of 14 hypotheses in order to advance research.

The article constructs a gap in the literature by means of pointing to a specific topic field to which institutional theory apparently has not been applied. At the same time, the article addresses how concepts from institutional theory need to be altered in order to be a better fit for this particular field. The article is inspirational to those who have an interest in institutional theory, but scholars who are interested in engaging in interdisciplinary research may also benefit from this article. The article finds many gaps in the literature and combines institutional theory and ecology. The hypotheses are developed in the following four areas: (1) the incorporation of values into organizational sustainability (H1–2), (2) the study of institutions as distinct elements within systems (H3–8), (3) the study of institutions as distinct spheres (H9–10), and (4) the construction of paradigms that support organizational sustainability (H11–14). For scholars in institutional theory, the authors succeed in presenting avenues for future research.

Giovannucci, D. and Ponte, S. 2005. Standards as a new form of social contract? Sustainability initiatives in the coffee industry. *Food Policy*, **30(3): 284–301.**

The article focuses on standards of sustainability and the authors have a particular interest in voluntary and private standards, while most research, the article claims, focuses on mandatory (imposed by governments) technical standards. The article offers a useful but brief discussion in a footnote on the existence of different classifications existing in the standards literature; however, it's superficial and does not cite sources. Besides, there is little if any conceptual contribution in the article.

The article is an in-depth case-based study that uses the coffee industry and addresses four significant questions in relation to sustainability standards: (1) Are these standards effective in communicating information and creating new markets? (2) To what extent do they embed elements of collective and private interests? (3) Is sustainability content actually delivered to their intended beneficiaries? (4) What is the role of public policy in addressing standards' shortcomings? Although the authors devote a section to answering each question, the broad nature of the article inspires future research in these areas. In particular, it appears that there is a need for more conceptual contributions.

The authors make the interesting argument that there has been a change in the normative framework that socially responsible corporations use for social legitimacy; this has boosted the development of sustainability standards. This is caused by the shift from the age of national capitalism, in which the concept of market fairness is embedded in a normative framework generated mostly by government and labor unions towards the current age of global capitalism, to a new situation in which other actors such as NGOs, industry associations and public–private partnerships provide the normative framework in which socially responsible corporations seek social legitimacy.

Therefore, corporations come to depend much more on standards that are developed outside the realm of the regular rule-makers (governments). The authors further suggest that this might be an advantage for producers if they are included in the standard-setting process, and in this sense sustainability 'systems could provide a more equitable forum for governing relations and activities along the value chain than what is provided through the market alone' (p. 298). This argument may very well be the starting point for more research into the composition of actors in standardizations work.

The article is interesting and poses timely questions as supported by researchers who have been studying standards as a phenomenon (e.g., Brunsson, Powell). Its broad questions make it a great discussion paper. The questions raised in this article may arise again in a more focused manner while using a different empirical perspective as well.

REVIEWS BY NATALIE SLAWINSKI

Lewis, D. 2003. NGOs, organizational culture, and institutional sustainability. *Annals of the American Academy of Political and Social Science*, **590(1): 212–26.**

This paper uses a qualitative approach to examine how the organizational culture of NGOs can reveal the complex roots of sustainability problems that exist in multi-agency rural development projects. Using the context of a sericulture (silk production) project in Bangladesh, the author finds that several initial project meanings have fragmented over time, thus contributing to a deeper understanding of some of the challenges of development. This paper is interesting in that it exposes the complexities of development by examining the relationship between organizational culture and sustainability, particularly in relation to the roles of NGOs and grassroots groups within such projects.

This paper challenges the dominant view of NGOs as a unitary group of organizations with similar characteristics. By examining the differences in ideology, scale, approach and culture of NGOs, Lewis extends research on organizational culture to the domain of NGOs – an area that is understudied. The author also challenges the technocratic worldview expressed by development planners that neglects the reality that NGOs are sociocultural systems embedded in wider social and political environments. This paper thus presents a more nuanced view of NGOs and opens the so-called black box.

Lewis gives a thorough overview of the organizational culture literature and then draws primarily on Handy's (1988) typology of cultures as club culture (most common within the NGO sector), role culture, task culture and person culture. He also discusses three levels of culture: (1) visible representation; (2) group behaviour; (3) underlying beliefs. Lewis argues that management writers have oversimplified the idea of organizational culture and he proposes to go into more depth by examining organizational culture as a process rather than as a set of outcomes.

Lewis develops case studies of multiple NGOs that are part of one sericulture project in Bangladesh. While this methodological approach is appropriate given the focus on organizational culture, the methods are not well described or transparent, making it difficult to understand how the author reached his observation that one of the NGOs had a role culture while the other had a person culture. Although it is interesting that the author finds differences in the NGOs, the lack of explanation leads one to question these findings and leaves much ambiguity. Using case studies also limits the generalizability of the findings.

Another shortcoming of the paper is that it does not review or define sustainability. The meaning that is used in the paper is that of being self-sustaining (able to exist without foreign aid). The author therefore assumes that there is only one meaning of sustainability without reviewing other definitions. Lewis's definition is very different from Rowlands' concept (see my review on Rowlands, 2001) of sustainability as resting on the three pillars of ecology, society and economy.

Lewis found that there is an incongruence between the market-based development values espoused by the World Bank (who sponsored the project) and the non-monetary values such as social solidarity espoused by some NGOs. Further research is needed into the above-mentioned incongruence. This tension may in fact stand in the way of project success and thus increase dependence on foreign aid, rather than reduce it.

The implication of this work for both managers and policy-makers (both governments and donors) is that they must understand the cultural diversity found within NGOs so as not to over-generalize the strengths and weaknesses of NGOs.

Reference

Handy, C. 1988. *Understanding Voluntary Organizations*. Harmondsworth: Penguin.

Oetzel, J. and Doh, J.P. 2009. MNEs and development: A review and reconceptualization. *Journal of World Business*, 44(2): 108–20.

This paper reviews two theories of international business and economics: the spillovers perspective that argues that MNEs contribute to the countries in which they operate through spillover effects (benefits that naturally accrue to local firms), and the liability of foreignness (LOF) perspective that argues that MNEs must overcome constraints in order to succeed in developing country markets. Because neither view gives a complete perspective on how MNEs and local economies can both benefit from foreign investment, the authors offer a third perspective – a resource complementarity perspective – in which MNEs and local NGOs collaborate to allow for social and economic development. This paper fills an important gap of highlighting the increasingly salient role played by local NGOs in MNE investments in developing countries.

The authors set out to answer two related research questions. In the first, they examine what the prominent theories in the international business (IB) literature suggest about the role of MNEs in host country development. Second, they ask whether collaboration between MNEs and NGOs can offer a more promising approach for promoting economic development in developing host countries. The authors begin by reviewing the two theories they consider most prominent: the spillovers and LOF perspectives. In doing so, the authors reveal each theory's conceptual and practical limitations in an era in which MNEs are under increasing pressure to make positive contributions to host country development. They challenge some of the existing orthodoxies in both the IB and economics literature, including the assumption that MNEs benefit host countries simply through their presence in those countries. They then offer a new perspective that draws attention to an oft-ignored, yet important, actor in the IB literature: NGOs.

The authors give a thorough account of both perspectives. The spillovers perspective has been critiqued for largely ignoring the developing world, and focusing instead on Triad countries (the US, Western Europe and Japan). Furthermore, the developed world along with institutions such as the World Trade Organization promote economic efficiency goals, such as global markets, which stand to benefit MNEs, often at the expense of developing country concerns. In addition, the empirical evidence of spillover effects such as technology transfer and knowledge transfer is weak at best, and there is evidence of negative economic, social and environmental spillovers from MNE activity. Finally, this view assumes that MNEs do not take an active role in trying to generate spillover benefits.

The authors also point out several weaknesses in the LOF perspective. For example, although there is evidence of social, political and economic costs associated with being a foreign firm, the LOF literature has emphasized short-term tactical solutions (such as hiring local staff) rather than long-term strategic solutions. This body of literature has also focused on Triad countries entering other Triad countries. Research on the base of the pyramid (BOP) has sought to redress this gap by focusing on developing countries, but the emphasis of this research has been on the benefits to the MNE rather than to the developing country.

Given these gaps in existing IB and international economics theories, the authors propose that MNEs can indeed create long-term benefits and sustainable social and economic development in their host countries, through partnerships with local NGOs. Here, the authors draw on the alliance literature, which has traditionally focused on corporate partnerships, rather than on MNE–NGO partnerships. This approach directs attention away from the perception that MNEs' and NGOs' values are inherently incompatible. Indeed, both MNEs and NGOs offer something of value to each other. MNEs offer size, scale, experience and resources, while NGOs offer MNEs access to important stakeholders. Together, these two organizational forms may enable institutional voids that often exist in developing countries to be filled. Table 1 is very helpful for sorting through the different perspectives and how the authors' new perspective fills gaps left by the existing theories.

This new approach, which the authors call 'a resource complementarity perspective', is a useful start to moving towards a theory that explores the mutual benefits for MNEs and developing countries rather than pitting the two against each other or assuming that MNEs by default offer benefits to host countries. However, the problem with this 'win–win' approach is that it does not go into enough depth on some of the many challenges and tensions that exist when MNEs and NGOs try to collaborate. It also ignores other tensions such as those between NGOs and local governments that may put MNEs in a difficult position.

The paper has both managerial and policy implications. Managers of MNEs can benefit from investing in the long-term growth and prosperity of developing countries. Policy-makers addressing development challenges in emerging markets can look to MNE–NGO collaboration as an alternative and innovative approach to development.

This paper offers a solid start to developing new theories that can better explain the role of MNEs in developing countries. The authors intend to stimulate research on the contribution of MNEs to the social and economic progress of developing host countries. Future research should also examine opportunities and challenges posed by MNE–NGO collaborations.

Rowlands, I.H. 2001. The Kyoto Protocol's 'Clean Development Mechanism': A sustainability assessment. *Third World Quarterly*, **22(5): 795–811.**

This paper assesses the Kyoto Protocol's Clean Development Mechanism (CDM) whereby developed countries can earn credits by abating greenhouse gas (GHG) emissions in developing countries. The author uses sustainability criteria (having ecological, economic and social dimensions) to evaluate key debates about CDM. By using all three dimensions, this paper assesses which approaches are best for people (reducing poverty and enhancing social equity), the planet (reducing environmental harm) and the economy (enhancing economic efficiency). Although there is no panacea, it represents an important tool for trying to achieve a balance of interests without displacing problems. It also demonstrates that setting restrictions on CDMs can encourage technology innovations in the long term, even if it may reduce economic efficiency in the short term. Given that the ability to adapt to climate change hinges on a portfolio of strategic options, the author suggests that a long-term approach to CDM that encourages the development of new technologies may be best for sustainability.

Since 1997, when the terms of the Kyoto Protocol were agreed upon by representatives from around the world, debate has ensued over the best way to implement CDMs. The author argues that given the controversy and complexity surrounding CDM, it needs to be assessed using objective criteria. Rowlands therefore develops criteria to determine CDM's consequences for sustainability, such that the pros and cons of CDM can be better understood and its complexities brought to the surface. In doing so, this paper provides a much-needed objective analysis to an ideologically driven debate about whether CDM should be restricted or not.

Rowlands gives a thorough overview of the two opposing views dominating the debate. The first view argues that CDM should not be restricted and that the market should allow for maximum efficiencies to emerge. The second view argues that CDM should be restricted to prevent developed countries and firms from over-using the often cheaper developing markets to meet their emissions objectives.

The author argues that objective criteria are needed to assess CDM, and proposes that sustainability criteria be used. He therefore reviews the sustainability literature and comes up with three common elements to many definitions: that sustainability rests upon the simultaneous consideration of social, ecological and economic goals. This overview of sustainability from the perspective of political science may be useful to organizational scholars in that it demonstrates that similar ambiguity exists in other disciplines surrounding the concept of sustainability.

Rowlands develops an assessment tool that seeks to measure the costs and benefits of each approach to CDM. He uses a 'make it the least bad approach', which compares the prospective impacts of CDM with slight variations on the same policy, rather than comparing CDM with other approaches. This approach allows the author to examine the different views of CDM to determine the strengths and weaknesses of each view and to determine objectively how CDM policy should proceed.

Three outstanding issues of CDM are assessed using the above tool: supplementarity, project eligibility and geographical quotas. Supplementarity refers to the decision regarding how much action on climate change should be required to occur 'at home' vs 'abroad'. Given that reducing emissions in developing countries is usually cheaper because this often involves incremental options like retrofitting, this may prevent firms from developing next-generation technologies that are needed to significantly reduce GHGs. Although it may seem more economically efficient in the short term, Rowlands concludes that a lack of restrictions is not the best solution from a sustainability standpoint in the long term.

Project eligibility refers to the decision regarding which projects should be allowed to operate under the CDM. Using the same tool, the author argues that a lack of restrictions on projects can lead to the problem of displacement. Firms may opt for a project that reduces GHGs but causes other environmental problems.

Geographical quotas are used to decide on the number of countries in which firms must invest. Most firms have focused their efforts to date on India and China where it is more economically efficient to engage in CDM projects. However, having more CDM projects in Africa and other developing countries would give more countries access to economic development. Therefore, quotas may be a better option in the long term.

The paper's most interesting finding is that imposing restrictions upon CDM has the most benefits for ecology and society while having no restrictions on CDM creates more short-term economic benefits. This presents an interesting dilemma for policy-makers who are often elected to a short time-frame but whose decisions will have long-term implications. They may want to select the best course of action for the long term but be constrained by their short electoral cycles, and the short-term interests of the constituents.

The paper does have several weaknesses. It presents an interesting tool to be used by managers and policy-makers when evaluating projects such as CDM, but does not discuss how this tool contributes to existing theory. Instead, the paper seems targeted solely at policy-makers, and the author does not discuss the tool's applicability beyond CDM. While the paper may not be generalizable beyond CDM, future research could apply the tool to other policy debates.

This paper has several managerial and policy implications. Although Rowlands does not discuss this, managers can use a similar tool when evaluating their climate change strategy. In terms of policy implications, governments can use this tool to understand the consequences of the different approaches to CDM.

REVIEWS BY SUSAN L. YOUNG

Starik, M. and Rands, G.P. 1995. Weaving an integrated web: Multilevel and multisystem perspectives of ecologically sustainable organizations. *Academy of Management Review*, **20(4): 908–35.**

This article explores the concept of ecological sustainability and applies it to organizations by utilizing a systems framework involving multiple levels of analysis. It also coins the term 'Ecologically Sustainable Organization' (ESO). There doesn't seem to be a specific research question being addressed; instead, this article seeks to clarify what is meant by ecological sustainability and then develops a multilevel framework through which ecological sustainability may be examined. These levels include: the individual, organizational, political-economic, social-cultural and ecological. This approach allows for a comprehensive examination of the ESO phenomenon.

As an *AMR* piece, there are no empirics to be found in this article. The authors pull from a few theoretical bases, such as open systems theory (Scott, 1992), the notion of fit (Drazin and Van de Ven, 1985) and the 'strategic-choice perspective' (Child, 1972), 'in which managers are boundedly rational (March and Simon, 1958) and are influenced by their values' (Starik and Rands, 1995, p. 915). It would be interesting to see if and how their argument would change if approached from a transaction cost economics (TCE) perspective (Williamson, 1979, 1985) that also considers bounded rationality but adds opportunism into the mix. Stakeholder theory[1] (Freeman, 1984) would also be an interesting theoretical basis to use, as it would bring in other important and possibly conflicting viewpoints other than just the needs of the ecological environment and the organization itself (although, frankly, the needs of the organization are under-represented as well). Likewise, either stream of institutional theory may be used – that of Scott (1995) and DiMaggio and Powell (1983) or the TCE-based new institutional economics (North, 1990) – both consider the greater institutional environment in which the firm operates, particularly the regulatory environment (of special importance here, with regards to the ecological environment).

The authors argue that 'as ecosystems provide the foundations of existence for both biological entities and organizations, sustainability of ecosystems must have higher priority than the economic sustainability of specific organizations' (p. 910). This is an interesting argument to find in a management journal such as *AMR*. In fact, throughout the article the *organization* is stressed, rather than the firm or business enterprise. The authors continue 'we assume, however, that the sustainability of both is possible and desirable'. This is a rather strong assumption to make – that is, that such mutual sustainability is possible. A natural extension of this article would be to take this argument further, examining whether the sustainability of both is indeed possible, or if trade-offs are necessary. While the actions of organizations in general are important in the institutional environment in which the firm is immersed, it is the actions of the economic entity of the *firm* that is the focus of the Academy of Management. The corporate social responsibility (CSR) literature is rife with economic arguments for and against CSR behavior by the firm, including ecological CSR (see Friedman, 1970; Davis, 1973; Preston and Post, 1981 for examples) – this literature could be enriched as well by extending these arguments into the sustainability literature.

The authors also draw our attention to the confusion that arises through the various definitions of ecological sustainability and propose their own: 'ecological sustainability is the ability of one or more entities, either individually or collectively, to exist and flourish (either unchanged or in evolved forms) for lengthy time-frames, in such a manner that the existence and growth of other collectivities of entities is permitted at related levels and in related systems' (p. 909). This definition is perhaps unnecessarily unwieldy and could be revisited by other theorists.

Rather than following a common format and using propositions to suggest what factors comprise ESOs, the authors make a series of declarative statements about how an ESO would be expected to act (or characteristics it would possess). These declarative statements can be found throughout the article, in italics (for example): '*ESOs will use natural resources no faster than either (1) rates of renewal, (2) rates of recycling, or (3) rates at which ecosystems' regenerative capacities will not have been exceeded by the time technological change and conversion to sustainable resources has occurred*' (p. 917). Any or several of these statements at each level of analysis could be rephrased as hypotheses and tested empirically to determine if ESOs truly exist as described here. More hypotheses could also be developed to determine if it is indeed economically possible or even feasible for firms to be ESOs. A comparison piece examining firms vs. other types of organizations (NGOs, non-profits, etc.) would be interesting, although a measure of performance would have to be carefully determined.

Finally, the authors themselves identify (pp. 929–30) several possible future questions raised by their framework:

> What are sustainable organizational rates of utilization of different natural resources? How do or can managers make these determinations? How do these rates, and their calculation, change as either technology or behavior changes? To what extent are natural resources substitutable amongst one another and

with other types of resources? What short-term variations in natural resource use rates are possible within long-term sustainable ranges? What feedback mechanisms can guide managers who will make these decisions?. . . What particular mix of financial and nonfinancial incentives should be offered to influence employees' sustainability-oriented behavior? In what amounts, at what time intervals, and for what particular behaviors should these incentives be offered? To what extent should organizational environmental policies reward compliance versus innovation?. . . In what ways, for example, will initiation and involvement in environmental partnerships be affected by differences in an organization's history, scale, sector, location, environmental munificence, and core competencies? How will differences in organizational and national culture, functional backgrounds, and reward systems influence the design and effectiveness of systems designed to sense and interpret negative/pro-sustainability feedback?

Building on the authors' framework, this article provides a launching point from which to more fully examine the issue of ecological sustainability in several directions particularly within each of the many levels the authors have utilized. A human resources/organizational behavior scholar, for example, might prefer to further examine the individual and organizational levels, while an international business (IB) or strategy-oriented scholar may prefer the political-economic, social-cultural and ecological levels. While the implications of differing cultural backgrounds are mentioned (p. 927), there is very little IB to be found in this article – this leaves the topic ripe for exploration by IB scholars (particularly the literature on culture – Kluckhohn and Strodtbeck, 1961; Hofstede, 1980 etc.). There is also mention of 'green marketing' (p. 925) – perhaps the marketing scholars can make use of this framework in their literature as well.

All in all, while this article has a few points that could arguably use some improvement such as the awkward definition of ecological sustainability and the use of declarative statements dictating the behavior of ESOs rather than challengeable propositions, it does provide a comprehensive framework that future scholars can build upon. Not only can the theory be further developed, there is great opportunity for empirical exploration as well.

Note

1. While Freeman (1984) is referenced (on p. 928), stakeholder theory is not used to any real extent within the article.

References

Child, J. 1972. Organizational structure, environment, and performance: The role of strategic choice. *Sociology*, **6**(1): 2–22.

Davis, K. 1973. The case for and against business assumption of social responsibilities. *Academy of Management Journal*, **16**(2): 312–22.

DiMaggio, P.J. and Powell, W.W. 1983. The iron cage revisited: Institutional isomorphism and collective rationality in organizational fields. *American Sociological Review*, **48**(2): 147–60.

Drazin, R. and Van de Ven, A.H. 1985. Alternative forms of fit in contingency theory. *Administrative Science Quarterly*, **30**(4): 514–39.

Freeman, R.E. 1984. *Strategic Management: A Stakeholder Approach*. Boston: Pittman.

Friedman, M. 1970. The social responsibility of business is to increase its profits. *New York Times Magazine*, 13 September: 32–3, 122, 124, 126.

Hofstede, G. 1980. *Culture's Consequences*. Beverly Hills, CA: Sage Publishing.

Kluckhohn, F.R. and Strodtbeck, F.L. 1961. *Variations in Value Orientations*. Oxford: Row, Peterson.

March, J.G. and Simon, H.A. 1958. *Organizations*. New York: Wiley.

North, D.C. 1990. *Institutions, Institutional Change and Economic Performance*. Cambridge: Cambridge University Press.

Preston, L.E. and Post, J.E. 1981. Private management and public policy. *California Management Review*, **23**(3): 56–62.

Scott, W.R. 1992. *Organizations: Rational, Natural, and Open Systems* (3rd edn). Englewood Cliffs, NJ: Prentice Hall.

Scott, W.R. 1995. *Institutions and Organization*. Thousand Oaks, CA: Sage Publishing.

Williamson, O.E. 1979. Transaction-cost economics: the governance of contractual relations. *The Journal of Law and Economics*, **22**(2): 233–61.

Williamson, O.E. 1985. The economics of organization: The transaction cost approach. *American Journal of Sociology*, **87**(3), 548–77.

Teegen, H., Doh, J.P. and Vachani, S. 2004. The importance of nongovernmental organizations (NGOs) in global governance and value creation: an international business research agenda. *Journal of International Business Studies*, **35**(6): 463–83.

This article contrasts non-governmental organizations (NGOs) with their private-sector (firm) and public-sector (government) counterparts within the context of international business (IB) research. The research question this article seeks to answer is this: what is the role and what are the functions of NGOs in global value creation? In order to explore this question the authors discuss the 'factors giving rise to NGOs as important organizational entities that participate in global value creation and governance, and identify limits to their efficacy and viability' (p. 463). Of particular relevance to the field of IB, they 'challenge three basic tenets of IB theory: the definition and dynamics of an institutional field, the relevance/centrality of a firm–government (i.e., two-sector) bargaining model, and the pre-eminence of the firm as the global organization of interest within the field' (p. 463). In IB, the contextual elements of the institutional environment in which the multinational enterprise (MNE) operates are particularly important. This makes the focus of this article a useful contribution to the IB literature.

This is a perspective piece in *JIBS* and therefore not empirical in nature. The authors begin with some useful definitions of what they term the 'third key set of players in value creation and governance' (Teegan et al., 2004, p. 464) – NGOs – and the non-profit sector, or 'civil society'. They take their working definition of NGOs from a United Nations (2003) description (although they streamline it considerably): 'NGOs are private, not-for-profit organizations that aim to serve particular societal interests by focusing advocacy and/or operational efforts on social, political and economic goals, including equity, education, health, environmental protection and human rights' (p. 466). They are looking in particular at 'social purpose NGOs', which are deemed accountable to the 'clients' they serve, distinctly different from 'membership' or 'club' NGOs that tend to 'promote the material, social, or political interests of their own members' (p. 466). Investigating the impact of these so-called 'club' NGOs – that would also impact the institutional context in which the MNE operates (as well as the domestic firm) – is one possible research topic.

The article further subdivides the social purpose NGO category into advocacy NGOs, operational NGOs and hybrid NGOs. Their discussion of advocacy NGOs lends itself easily to an examination of institutional voids (though this is not the language used) that could be further addressed through the support of new institutional economics theory (North, 1990). Another potential theoretical approach could be stakeholder theory (Freeman, 1984), particularly if exploring their discussion of 'insider' vs. 'outsider' strategies, where 'insider' strategies are aimed at influencing decision-makers directly and 'outsider' strategies are intended to mobilize public opinion (Peterson, 1992). Regarding their consideration of operational NGOs, once again the concept of institutional voids arises through their discussion of failed markets. Here a transaction cost economics theory approach (Coase, 1937; Williamson, 1975, 1985) might provide a richer exploration of the concepts raised.

The authors discuss the rise of NGOs in the global context, explaining how 'several historical and political developments help to explain the increased presence and importance of NGOs on the world stage' (pp. 469–70). This leads to the coining of another term: international non-governmental organizations (INGOs). Underlying the article's outline of specific historical and political developments is a question of legitimization. However, this term is not used nor is this concept examined except to acknowledge that these significant events 'signal official recognition of the growing importance of NGOs' (Teegan et al., 2004, p. 469). Future scholars could certainly explore the concept of legitimization of NGOs with much greater depth. The reputation literature could be of benefit here, as could institutional theory (DiMaggio and Powell, 1983; Scott, 1995). This could be examined from both micro (human resources/organizational behavior) and macro (strategy/IB) viewpoints; there may be empirical opportunities here as well.

Like the Weidenbaum (2009) article, this paper calls into question the relative 'immunity from transparency' (Hayden, 2002; Florini, 2003) from which NGOs benefit. This is an area that calls for further scholarly examination. The corporate governance literature, from either/both a management and a financial discipline point of view, could be helpful here. (See my Weidenbaum, 2009 review for further suggestions.)

The authors propose a future research agenda of their own: one that calls into question the traditional IB assumption that posits 'states at the center of governance and firms at the center of value creation (Mathews, 1997; Smith et al., 1997; Simmons, 1998; Robertson, 2000)' (Teegan et al., 2004, p.472). Using their model that acknowledges the definitive existence of the third sector (civil society), represented by the NGO, challenges and expands the boundaries that define the context in which the MNE operates. 'NGOs have the potential to dramatically alter traditional conceptions of the role of MNEs in the global economy and their relations with other players. This is especially true for the bargaining relationship between MNEs and host governments that historically has been conceived as primarily bilateral in nature (Kobrin, 1987; Vernon, 1971; Vachani, 1995)' (Teegan et al., 2004, p.475). Including the importance of a third sector has the potential to alter Vernon's bargaining model, if not negate it completely.

By acknowledging the effect NGOs can have and the constraints they can place on MNE behavior with regards to global governance and value creation, this proposed three-sector framework requires a re-examination of several basic IB tenets – including the definition of MNE itself. The authors suggest that the NGO could fit the very definition of MNE: 'NGOs, which are also private (i.e., non-state) actors, also create value – both social and economic' (p.476). The MNE lies at the very heart of IB – re-examination of this definition could have repercussions throughout IB theory. This notion deserves further exploration. In order to test this supposition the authors propose scholars revisit various theories of the MNE, using the NGO in place of the MNE, and see if the logic still holds. One theory that could receive such treatment is Dunning's (1988) eclectic (OLI) paradigm, suggesting that INGOs may also leverage ownership, location and internationalization factors 'to engage successfully in global settings' (Teegan et al., 2004, p.476) much as MNEs do. Vernon's (1966) life cycle theory could be re-examined in this way, as could theories of internationalization (i.e., Johanssen and Vahlne, 1977; Lindenberg and Bryant, 2001). Any theory used in IB could be renewed. In the authors' own words, 'it is difficult for us to conceive of an IB theory regarding

MNEs that *a priori* would be deemed irrelevant to international NGOs as value-creating MNEs' (p. 477).

The authors do acknowledge that MNE performance is typically judged by profitability and that 'different performance metrics will have to be devised for international NGOs (Brinkerhoff et al., 2003)' (Teegan et al., 2004, p. 477). Empirical experts might find this a worthy challenge.

It should be emphasized that the impact of NGOs (or INGOs) is not a strictly IB issue; many disciplines could benefit from further exploration of this topic. For example, 'even issues such as human resource management and organizational behavior in culturally diverse settings are germane to international NGOs (Hailey and Smillie, 2001; Lewis, 2002) (Teegan et al., 2004, p. 477). Recognizing the importance of 'civil society' to the institutional environment in which the firm operates and incorporating NGOs into future models will serve to enrich our understanding of the firm's interactions within this environment, for all business scholars, not just IB scholars. NGOs should be considered a universal phenomenon that deserves our attention.

References

Brinkerhoff, J.M., Smith, S.C. and Teegen, H. 2003. On the role and efficacy of NGOs in achieving the Millennium Development Goals: A framework for analysis and assessment, George Washington University INGOT Working Paper No. 1.

Coase, R.H. 1937. The nature of the firm. *Economica*, **4**(16): 386–405.

DiMaggio, P.J. and Powell, W.W. 1983. The iron cage revisited: Institutional isomorphism and collective rationality in organizational fields. *American Sociological Review*, **48**(2): 147–60.

Dunning, J.H. 1988. The eclectic paradigm of international production: A restatement and some possible extensions. *Journal of International Business Studies*, **19**(1): 1–31.

Florini, A. 2003. *The Coming Democracy: New Rules for Running a New World*. Washington, DC: Island Press.

Freeman, R.E. 1984. *Strategic Management: A Stakeholder Approach*. Boston: Pittman.

Hailey, J. and Smillie, I. 2001. *Managing for Change: Leadership, Strategy, and Management in Asian NGOs*. London: Earthscan Publications.

Hayden, R. 2002. Dictatorships of virtue? *Harvard International Review*, **24**(2): 56–61.

Johanssen, J. and Vahlne, J.-E. 1977. The internationalization process of the firm – a model of knowledge development and increasing foreign market commitments. *Journal of International Business Studies*, **8**(1): 23–32.

Kobrin, S.J. 1987. Testing the bargaining hypothesis in the manufacturing sector in developing countries. *International Organization*, **41**(4): 609–38.

Lewis, D. 2002. Organization and management in the third sector: Toward a cross-cultural research agenda. *Nonprofit Management and Leadership*, **13**(1): 67–83.

Lindenberg, M. and Bryant, C. 2001. *Going Global: Transforming Relief and Development NGOs*. West Hartford, CT: Kumarian Press.

Mathews, J.T. 1997. Power shift. *Foreign Affairs*, **76**(1): 50–66.

North, D.C. 1990. *Institutions, Institutional Change and Economic Performance*. Cambridge: Cambridge University Press.

Peterson, M.J. 1992. Transnational activity, international society and world politics. *Millennium: Journal of International Studies*, **21**(3): 371–88.

Robertson, D. 2000. Civil society and the WTO. *The World Economy*, **23**(9): 1119–34.

110 *Research companion to green international management studies*

Scott, W.R. 1995. *Institutions and Organization.* Thousand Oaks, CA: Sage Publishing.
Simmons, P.J. 1998. Learning to live with NGOs. *Foreign Policy*, **112**(Fall): 82–96.
Smith, J., Chatfield, C. and Pagnucco, R. (eds). 1997. *Transnational Social Movements and Global Politics: Solidarity Beyond the State.* Syracuse, NY: Syracuse University Press.
United Nations. 2003. NGO committee concludes 2002 resumed session, with final recommendations on economic and social council consultative status. Available at http://www.in.org/News/Press/docs/2003/ngo494.doc.htm; accessed 7 February 2003.
Vachani, S. 1995. Enhancing the obsolescing bargain theory: A longitudinal study of foreign ownership of US and European multinationals. *Journal of International Business Studies*, **26**(1): 159–80.
Vernon, R. 1966. International investment and international trade in the product life cycle. *Quarterly Journal of Economics*, **80**(2): 190–207.
Vernon, R. 1971. *Sovereignty at Bay: The Multinational Spread of US Enterprise.* New York: Basic Books.
Weidenbaum, M. 2009. Who will guard the guardians? The social responsibility of NGOs. *Journal of Business Ethics*, **87**(1): 147–55.
Williamson, O.E. 1975. *Markets and Hierarchies: Analysis and Antitrust Implications.* New York: Free Press.
Williamson, O.E. 1985. The economics of organization: The transaction cost approach. *American Journal of Sociology*, **87**(3): 548–77.

Weidenbaum, M. 2009. Who will guard the guardians? The social responsibility of NGOs. *Journal of Business Ethics*, 87(1): 147–55.

The primary research question of this article is: to whom are non-governmental organizations (NGOs) responsible? This is actually a very important question; NGOs themselves attempt to hold businesses and other institutions socially responsible for their actions, yet NGOs 'rarely have established governance mechanisms whereby their members and supporters can hold them [NGOs] accountable for their activities' (Weidenbaun, 2009, p. 147). This article has therefore spotlighted a significant disconnect present in the contextual environment in which a firm operates. However, it should be noted that this article concerns itself principally with this disconnect between an NGO's stated concern of focus on the social accountability of firms and other institutions while not having to accept scrutiny themselves, rather than the effect of this disconnect on the environment surrounding the firm and the behavior of the firm itself. A concentration on the effect on the business environment, rather than leaving it to the realm of public policy, would be a rich question for business scholars.

The article itself states that 'the important contributions of NGOs to public policy' (ibid.) are not at issue here, but rather the focus is on the narrower question of governance. The author calls for a reformation in the governance of NGOs in light of their particular contributions to society, and towards the end of the article imparts a practical list of governance reforms that can be enacted, drawn from previous work by others. No particular suggestion is preferred. In general, this article has a very practical bent and despite appearing in an academic journal appears to be geared more towards the practitioner than the academic.

This propensity towards the practical does not negate the importance of the underlying research question, but the article does beg for a more theoretical basis for its argument. Considering that the focus of this article is on governance, pulling from the financial academic arena may be helpful. Another approach could involve examining the effect of the disconnect mentioned above on the context of the business environment that could then pull from institutional theory (DiMaggio and Powell, 1983; Scott, 1995) or new institutional economics (North, 1990). If taking a strategy approach, agency theory (Jensen and Meckling, 1976) would be a good theory to draw from, particularly beginning with Fama and Jensen (1983) on how the separation of residual risk-bearing from decision management leads to separation of decision management (initiation and implementation) from decision control (ratification and monitoring). The Fama and Jensen article addresses different types of organizations including non-profits; examination of NGOs in the same vein could extend this literature. Another academic direction would be to extend this question across international borders and examine differences in the governance structures of NGOs originating from different nations. This approach could draw from the institutional theories as well, or from a cultural angle (Kluckhohn and Strodtbeck, 1961; Hofstede, 1980; Ronen and Shenkar, 1985), for starters.

There are some empirics used in this article to support the claim that NGOs have, generally speaking, little governance and oversight established for their basic decision-making processes and operations. The sample consists of 34 consumer advocacy organizations taken by the Weidenbaum Center at Washington University in the spring of 2007 and are listed in Table 1. The empirics themselves consist of a simple yes/no count of (1) whether supporters vote for board members and (2) whether supporters vote on the agenda of the NGO. The author freely admits that this sample is of a limited nature, and does not try to go beyond simple statistics. One area for future research is to extend this example into a true examination of the governance structures of NGOs. A more comprehensive analysis of NGO governance structures is preferable that would require a more elaborate data set with more variables – one that allows for control variables for a more rigorous examination. A suggestion would be to follow in the footsteps of Zajac and Westphal (1994) who examined the effect of types of board membership on corporate monitoring by the board of directors (many NGOs have boards of directors as well). For example, Zajac and Westphal demonstrated that firms with (1) a larger percentage of outside directors on their boards, (2) a larger percentage of director stock ownership, (3) a major non-board member blockholder (who owns at least 5 percent of the common stock), and (4) a separate CEO/Board Chairman position are more likely to have greater corporate monitoring (ibid.). The empirical methodology used by Zajac and Westphal involving pooled cross-sectional time series regression (Sayrs, 1989) may be appropriate for examining NGO boards, given the proper data set. Another research opportunity could also involve using an international data set.

In general, this article has raised an interesting research question regarding the lack of accountability of NGOs, particularly ironic in light of the aim of NGOs to hold *other* institutions accountable for *their* actions. However, this article is not very empirically rigorous nor is it theoretically strong. The article appears to be targeted at the practitioner, not the academic; it's a future research opportunity – academics may engage in a more thorough exploration. In addition, the article does not consider other related literature appropriately or adequately, allowing for further examination of the primary question through many possible theoretical lenses. Some suggestions for such further exploration and extension are offered throughout this review. In employing some of these suggestions, it is hoped that not only can scholars more fully examine the initial research question raised by this article, but also that such research will uncover even more evocative questions in the process.

References

DiMaggio, P.J. and Powell, W.W. 1983. The iron cage revisited: Institutional isomorphism and collective rationality in organizational fields. *American Sociological Review*, **48**(2): 147–60.
Fama, E.F. and Jensen M.C. 1983. Separation of ownership and control. *Journal of Law and Economics*, **26**(2): 301–25.
Hofstede, G. 1980. *Culture's Consequences*. Beverly Hills, CA: Sage Publishing.
Jensen, M.C. and Meckling, W.H. 1976. Theory of the firm: Managerial behavior, agency costs, and ownership structure. *Journal of Financial Economics*, **3**(4): 305–50.
Kluckhohn, F.R. and Strodtbeck, F.L. 1961. *Variations in Value Orientations*. Oxford: Row, Peterson.
North, D.C. 1990. *Institutions, Institutional Change and Economic Performance*. Cambridge: Cambridge University Press.
Ronen, S. and Shenkar, O. 1985. Clustering countries on attitudinal dimensions: A review and synthesis. *Academy of Management Review*, **10**(3): 435–54.
Sayrs, L.W. (1989). *Pooled Time Series Analysis*. London: Sage Publishing.
Scott, W.R. 1995. *Institutions and Organizations*. Thousand Oaks, CA: Sage Publishing.
Zajac, E.J. and Westphal, J.D. 1994. The costs and benefits of managerial incentives and monitoring in large U.S. corporations: When is more not better? *Strategic Management Journal*, **15**(51): 121–42.

5 Environmental innovation and talent*
*Claire A. Simmers, Amanda Bullough,
Mary S. Finney, Dean Hennessy,
Laurie Ingraham and Olga Hawn*

OVERVIEW BY CLAIRE A. SIMMERS

The scope of the Environmental Innovation and Talent subfield of green international management studies centers on four key questions. The first question is, why, where, and how do firms incorporate environmental innovation and strategies? The second question is, what are the firm's talent, resources and competency needs for environmental innovation? The third question is how do external stakeholders impact environmental innovation? The fourth question is, how do multidisciplines and methods contribute to our understanding of environmental innovation?

The current state of the literature on why, where, and how firms incorporate environmental innovation strategies divides into four areas (Wiklund and Shepherd, 2003; Reinstaller, 2005; Chen, 2008; Horbach, 2008; Tello and Yoon, 2008; Del Río, 2009). Firms environmentally innovate because of supply-driven motivations, focusing on operational aspects aimed at extracting cost efficiencies. Demand motivations from customers and concerns for image drive firms to environmental innovation with marketing and product development initiatives at the forefront. Institutional and political influences also push firms towards environmental innovation, in products, processes and image. Firms address these influences mainly through corporate-driven responses in the appropriate areas. Finally, firms incorporate environmental innovation strategies because of co-evolutionary forces arising from interactions with multiple stakeholders such as suppliers and competitors. Any level in the firm can be the impetus for innovation, using techniques (e.g., cost cutting, process innovation, brand imaging) applicable to that level.

An important gap in the literature in the first question is definitional; there is no common terminology. Is it environmental innovation, is it sustainability, is it sustainable innovation, or is it green management? The

---

* Facilitator: Claire A. Simmers.

114   *Research companion to green international management studies*

lack of clarity and commonality in definitions cascades into inconsistency in theory application and construct usage and measurement, making conclusions across studies difficult. Another gap is theory development that encompasses the four drivers of innovation (supply, demand, institutional and co-evolutionary). Current theory does not address any synergistic interaction. The opportunities for research in this area are for construct development and theory development incorporating multiple research traditions.

The talents, resources and competencies needed (or lacking) in environmental innovation is a rich field for current research efforts (Larson, 2000; Wiklund and Shepherd, 2003; Laszlo et al., 2005; Reinstaller, 2005; Szekely and Knirsch, 2005; Chen, 2008; Lynes and Andrachuk, 2008; Kolk and Pinkse, 2008). Leadership, core competencies and the mental models and mindsets for environmental innovation are conceptually and empirically examined.

A gap in the literature offering an opportunity for future research is addressing, in a systematic way, the interaction of influences at the level of the firm. Many of the studies do not investigate how groups affect environmental innovation. There is a gap in our understanding of partnership skills necessary for successful environmental innovation, leading to the opportunity to examine how working together either across or within a firm contributes to environmental innovation.

The current state of the literature on the impact of external stakeholders on environmental innovation offers several points (Jaffe et al., 2005; Reinstaller, 2005; Szekely and Knirsch, 2005; Del Rio, 2009; Van Alphen et al., 2009). The external environment is usually vaguely defined as public policy. Whether innovation will progress or be deterred is dependent on who is in power at the time (Van Alphen et al., 2009). There is also evidence that policy entrepreneurs and NGOs initiate social pressure on firms for environmental innovation (Reinstaller, 2005). Not surprisingly, research finds evidence of a gap between what firms report on their environmental innovation efforts and the level of disclosure that stakeholders want and/ or need (Szekely and Knirsch, 2005). Major research gaps are (1) in the definition of external environment as it is too often limited in the current studies to public policy, (2) in longitudinal research on the role and impact of stakeholders, and (3) in studies across multiple national cultures. The gaps provide opportunities to research the role of different stakeholders through time and place as well as the commonalities, if any, across national cultures.

The fourth question is, how do multidisciplines and methods contribute to our understanding of environmental innovation? Current research uses entrepreneurship literature to study sustainable innovation (Larson, 2000) and strategy research on core competencies (Chen, 2008). The fields of economics (particularly incentives) and public policy (primarily duality and firm/policy interaction) provide insights on environmental innovation (Jaffe et al., 2005; Reinstaller, 2005; Del Rio, 2009). Current literature also suggests that patents are not a viable measure of environmental innovation (Wagner, 2007). The use of case studies and anecdotal evidence characterizes a portion of the current research (Lynes and Andrachuk, 2008; Thomson and Khare, 2008).

How we measure environmental innovation is a major gap. Another gap is the lack of research from traditions such as the social sciences that would help us understand individual motivations and skills facilitating or hindering environmental innovation. There is also a gap in the use and improvement of existing databases on environmental innovation. One opportunity for future research is to utilize several theoretical traditions, either in a comparative or integrative manner. Another opportunity for future research is to develop other variables aside from patents to measure environmental innovation.

References

Chen, Y. 2008. The driver of green innovation and green image: Green core competence. *Journal of Business Ethics*, **81**(3): 531–43.

Del Rio, P. 2009. The empirical analysis of the determinants for environmental technological change: A research agenda. *Ecological Economics*, **68**(3): 861–78.

Horbach, J.J. 2008. Determinants of environmental innovation: New evidence from German panel data sources. *Research Policy*, **37**(1): 163–73.

Jaffe, A.B., Newell, R.G. and Stavins, R.N. 2005. A tale of two market failures: Technology and environmental policy. *Ecological Economics*, **54**(2–3): 164–74.

Kolk, A. and Pinkse, J. 2008. A perspective on multinational enterprises and climate change: Learning from 'an inconvenient truth'? *Journal of International Business Studies*, **39**(8): 1359–78.

Larson, A.L. 2000. Sustainable innovation through an entrepreneurship lens. *Business Strategy and the Environment*, **9**(5): 304–17.

Laszlo, C., Sherman, D., Whalen, J. and Ellison, J. 2005. How stakeholder value contributes to competitive advantage. *Journal of Corporate Citizenship*, **20**: 65–76.

Lynes, J.K. and Andrachuk, M. 2008. Motivations for corporate social and environmental responsibility: A case study of Scandinavian Airlines. *Journal of International Management*, **14**(4): 377–90.

Reinstaller, A. 2005. Policy entrepreneurship in the co-evolution of institutions, preferences, and technology: Comparing the diffusion of totally chlorine free pulp bleaching technologies in the US and Sweden. *Research Policy*, **34**(9): 1366–84.

Szekely, F. and Knirsch, M. 2005. Responsible leadership and corporate social responsibility: Metrics for sustainable performance. *European Management Journal*, **23**(6): 628–47.

Tello, S.F. and Yoon, E. 2008. Examining drivers of sustainable innovation. *Journal of International Business Strategy*, **8**(3): 164–9.

Thomson, D. and Khare, A. 2008. Carbon capture and storage (CCS) deployment – can Canada capitalize on experience? *Journal of Technology Management and Innovation*, **3**(4): 111–18.

Van Alphen, K., Van Ruijven, J., Kasa, S., Hekkert, M. and Turkenburg,W. 2009. The performance of the Norwegian carbon dioxide, capture and storage innovation system. *Energy Policy*, **37**(2): 43–55.

Wagner, M. 2007. On the relationship between environmental management, environmental innovation and patenting: Evidence from German manufacturing firms. *Research Policy*, **36**(10): 1587–602.

Wiklund, J. and Shepherd, D. 2003. Knowledge-based resources, entrepreneurial orientation, and the performance of small and medium-sized businesses. *Strategic Management Journal*, **24**(13): 1307–14.

REVIEWS BY AMANDA BULLOUGH

Chen, Y. 2008. The driver of green innovation and green image: Green core competence. *Journal of Business Ethics*, **81(3): 531–43.**

This paper explores the positive effects that 'green core competences' can have on 'green' innovation and a firm's 'green' image. Companies have been compelled to engage in environmental protection activities to comply with regulations and appeal to environmentally conscious consumers (Hart, 1995, 1997; Berry and Rondinelli, 1998). Chen argues for multiple benefits resulting from green innovation: first mover advantages, green product differentiation, higher prices for green products, warding off of consumer backlash to irresponsible practices while promoting a positive corporate image and a further subsequent competitive advantage from these positive outcomes (Peattie, 1992; Porter and Van der Linde, 1995; Shrivastava, 1995; Chen et al., 2006).

Chen extends Prahalad and Hamel's (1990) concept of core competences to propose 'green core competences' by synthesizing literature from environmental management and corporate strategy. Based on a review of this literature, Chen hypothesized that green core competences will positively affect green product and process innovation performance. In addition, based on past research (i.e., Chan, 2000), Chen hypothesized that green core competences are positively related to green images, and in turn hypothesized that green product and process innovation performance would also have a positive association with a green image.

The firm-level study was conducted on data from information and electronics companies that produce pollution in Taiwan, randomly selected from the 2006 Taiwanese business directory. Those responding to the questionnaire were CEOs and managers of environmental protection, marketing or R&D departments.

A seven-point Likert scale questionnaire with a total of 21 items was designed and validated by expert and scholar modification. Then a random sample test group of respondents completed the questionnaire before it was fully administered. All four scales in the instrument were validated with strong Cronbach's alphas, and all items loaded squarely on their intended factors. The final sample size was 136, with 67 larger enterprises and 69 SMEs.

All hypotheses were supported by significant regression analysis results, highlighting the importance of green core competences on green image and on green innovation performance. These results also showcase the importance of green innovation performance on a company's green image.

In addition, Chen found that size matters – larger companies reap stronger benefits from these results than SMEs.

The hypotheses themselves were fairly well supported with prior research and the model proposed is strong and empirically testable. Unfortunately, the paper would benefit from some editing, especially to deal specifically with the repetitive nature of the literature review and the descriptions of the constructs being tested.

While it was an interesting finding that firm size was found to be a significant factor in the development of green core competences in Tawain's information and electronics industry, this finding may not be of value outside this industry or outside Taiwan. Additional future studies could seek to demonstrate wider generalizability. The important contributions to be gleaned from the empirical results are the positive effects of green core competences on innovation and image, regardless of firm size.

Finally, it might be interesting to run the analyses in reverse to see if the relationships go both ways. It may be possible that green core competences are built as a result of a positive green image and green innovation, instigated by changing environmental regulations and consumer expectations (Kolk and Pinkse, 2008).

References

Berry, M.A. and Rondinelli, D.A. 1998. Proactive corporate environmental management: A new industrial revolution. *Academy of Management Executive*, **12**(2): 38–50.

Chan, R.Y.K. 2000. The effectiveness of environmental advertising: The role of claim type and the source country green image. *International Journal of Advertising*, **19**(3): 349–75.

Chen, Y.-S., Lai, S.-B. and Wen, C.-T. 2006. The influence of green innovation performance on corporate advantage in Taiwan. *Journal of Business Ethics*, **67**(4): 331–9.

Hart, S.L. 1995. A natural-resource-based view of the firm. *Academy of Management Review*, **20**(4): 986–1014.

Hart, S.L. 1997. Beyond greening: Strategies for a sustainable world. *Harvard Business Review*, **75**(1): 67–76.

Kolk, A. and Pinkse, J. 2008. A perspective on multinational enterprises and climate change: Learning from 'An Inconvenient Truth'? *Journal of International Business Studies*, **39**(8): 1359–78.

Peattie, K. 1992. *Green Marketing*. London: Pitman Publishing.

Porter, M.E. and van der Linde, C. 1995. Green and competitive. *Harvard Business Review*, **73**(5): 120–34.

Prahalad, C.K. and Hamel, G. 1990. The core competence of the corporation. *Harvard Business Review*, **68**(3): 79–91.

Shrivastava, P. 1995. Environmental technologies and competitive advantage. *Strategic Management Journal*, **16**(Special issue): 183–200.

Kolk, A. and Pinkse, J. 2008. A perspective on multinational enterprises and climate change: Learning from 'An Inconvenient Truth'? *Journal of International Business Studies*, 39(8): 1359–78.

This article explores climate change and how it can offer opportunities to develop new firm-specific advantages (FSAs), or alter existing FSAs. Kolk and Pinske (2008) base a large part of their argument on prior work by Rugman and Verbeke (1998, 2000, 2001) and espouse that a new domain of research links corporate sustainability policy with societal sustainability for country-specific and firm-specific advantages. In other words, societal and corporate sustainability become intertwined. To do so, the article applies a resource-based view to sustainability in that resources will only be allocated if they will in turn lead to green FSAs. This depends on how well those resources can be leveraged in other ways and on the flexibility of reversing their usage if necessary. This becomes difficult when FSAs and country-specific advantages (CFAs) are out of alignment because of differing country-level environmental regulations.

Kolk and Pinske (2008) then extend Rugman and Verbeke's framework to explore how MNEs utilize FSAs to manage the global sustainability issue over time. This requires dynamic capabilities (Teece et al., 1997) in order to modify and adapt FSAs to remain responsive to CFAs, and learning capabilities to stay abreast of future developments. This paper specifically focuses on climate change to examine whether and how MNEs build new green FSAs or change key FSAs to be greener by applying two frameworks: the nature of FSA development and the geographic location of FSA development.

The nature of FSA development framework relates to specific capabilities and core competencies for any given company (Toyota hybrid cars and oil and gas companies). The argument made by Kolk and Pinske (2008) is that MNEs will most likely follow one of three avenues to green FSA development: capability evolution, capability transformation, or capability substitution (Lavie, 2006). The amount of commitment from the MNE to these endeavors depends on the potential spillover effects on the entire value chain, the upstream (supply end) of the value chain, or the downstream (customer end).

The geography of FSA development framework uses CSAs as the starting point for developing or nurturing FSAs at specific geographic locations within the corporation only – where climate change may pose a threat in one location, it may present an opportunity in another. With this framework, Kolk and Pinske (2008) argue that decision-making power will come from corporate headquarters, a regional center, or a national subsidiary based on the degree of transferability of the climate-induced

FSA – whether it is location-bound or not (see Figure 2 in Kolk and Pinske).

This conceptual paper was supported by a qualitative review of the Carbon Disclosure Project published in May 2004; Kolk and Pinske (2008) identify MNEs that have engaged in developing climate-induced FSAs. They then collected archival information from corporate sustainability reports, NGO and carbon consultant reports, and reviews in *The Financial Times*.

While this paper is current and poses an important research topic, it is also one of the first strategy papers to look at developing FSAs based on climate change. Future research is imperative, but data will be difficult to gather until more firms engage in such practices industrywide in order to collect comparative data. Kolk and Pinske (2008) highlight that their contribution to the field lies in the potential for managers to use this proposed framework when evaluating the risks and rewards of investing and developing FSAs. In addition, policy-makers can use the framework to better shape CSAs and then directly or indirectly influence firms to invest in FSAs. The authors conclude that climate-induced FSAs may lead to radical, competence-destroying FSAs for a few industries, like oil, gas and automotives, but this will happen slowly as long as companies disagree on technology.

References

Lavie, D. 2006. Capability reconfiguration: An analysis of incumbent responses to technological change. *Academy of Management Review*, **31**(1): 153–74.

Rugman, A.M. and Verbeke, A. 1998. Corporate strategies and environmental regulations: An organizing framework. *Strategic Management Journal*, **19**(4): 363–75.

Rugman, A.M. and Verbeke, A. 2000. Six cases of corporate strategic responses to environmental regulation. *European Management Journal*, **18**(4): 377–85.

Rugman, A.M. and Verbeke, A. 2001. Environmental policy and international business. In A.M. Rugman and T.L. Brewer (eds), *The Oxford Handbook of International Business*. Oxford: Oxford University Press, pp. 537–57.

Teece, D.J., Pisano, G. and Shuen, A. 1997. Dynamic capabilities and strategic management. *Strategic Management Journal*, **18**(7): 509–33.

Wiklund, J. and Shepherd, D. 2003. Knowledge-based resources, entrepreneurial orientation, and the performance of small and medium-sized businesses. *Strategic Management Journal*, 24(13): 1307–14.

Wiklund and Shepherd extend traditional resource-based research (Barney, 1991, 1995) to an examination of the relationship between resources and the way a firm is organized. The authors argue that a firm's entrepreneurial strategic orientation (EO) (Lumpkin and Dess, 1996) represents an important component of how a firm is organized.

Upon highlighting the importance of organizational knowledge for discovering and exploiting new opportunities, Wiklund and Shepherd focus specifically on procedural, market and technological knowledge for sustainable competitive advantage. They hypothesize that such knowledge-based resources, that lend to the discovery and exploitation of opportunities, are positively related to firm performance. The authors also argue that EO is comprised of innovativeness, proactiveness and risk-taking and hypothesize that because firms with EO focus attention and effort on opportunities, therefore EO is positively related to firm performance. Finally, the authors hypothesize that firms with strong knowledge-based resources, plus EO, will have even higher firm performance – EO moderates this relationship.

The sample used to test the hypotheses is comprised of 384 Swedish SME CEOs. Data for the independent and control variables were collected in 1997, and data for the dependent variable (i.e., firm performance) were collected in 2000, both via telephone and mail questionnaires. The *performance* dependent variable was based on a composite answer of ten performance dimensions. Five-point Likert scale questions were used to ask respondents to compare themselves on these dimensions to their two top competitors over the previous three years. Eleven items from a scale used by Gupta and Govindarajan (2000) were used to gather the firm knowledge independent variables. The EO independent variable consisted of Covin and Slevin's (1989) nine-item instrument. Wiklund and Shepherd also controlled for munificence (Dess and Beard's (1984) four-item scale), heterogeneity (Miller and Friesen's (1982) three-item scale), past performance (net profit, sales growth, cash flow and growth of net worth), firm age, firm size, industry effects (from the firm's main line of business in manufacturing, retail or service).

All hypotheses were supported. The findings of this research suggest that the knowledge-based resources necessary for the discovery and exploitation of opportunities are positively related to firm performance, and EO positively moderates this relationship. In other words, a firm's propensity to be innovative, proactive and risk-taking strengthens the benefits of knowledge-based resources on performance. Not only are the resources themselves important, but how the firm is organized and positioned to use and leverage those resources also has important implications for performance.

References

Barney, J. 1991. Firm resources and sustained competitive advantage. *Journal of Management*, **17**(1): 99–120.

Barney, J. 1995. Looking inside for competitive advantage. *Academy of Management Executive*, **9**(4): 49–61.

Covin, J.G. and Slevin, D.P. 1989. Strategic management of small firms in hostile and benign environments. *Strategic Management Journal*, **10**(1): 75–87.

Dess, G.G. and Beard, D.W. 1984. Dimensions of organizational task environments. *Administrative Science Quarterly*, **29**(1): 52–73.

Gupta, A. and Govindarajan, V. 2000. Knowledge flows within multinational corporations. *Strategic Management Journal*, **21**(4): 473–96.

Lumpkin, G.T. and Dess, G.G. 1996. Clarifying the entrepreneurial orientation construct and linking it to performance. *Academy of Management Review*, **21**(1): 135–72.

Miller, D. and Friesen, P.H. 1982. Innovation in conservative and entrepreneurial firms: Two models of strategic momentum. *Strategic Management Journal*, **3**(1): 1–25.

REVIEWS BY MARY S. FINNEY

Laszlo, C., Sherman, D., Whalen, J. and Ellison, J. 2005. How stakeholder value contributes to competitive advantage. *Journal of Corporate Citizenship*, **20**: 65–76.

Managers recognize their responsibility to deliver financial returns to their shareholders and yet, today they are increasingly called upon to balance this obligation with their responsibilities to society and the environment. This article not only provides a blueprint for corporations, but also succeeds in building an important bridge between the corporate and not-for-profit worlds by helping to break down the walls of misunderstanding. The authors offer a theory: stakeholder value, which they contend is based on the economic, environmental and social impacts a company has on its diverse constituents. They challenge managers to consider a deep rethinking about their business process.

Sustainable development and social responsibility are abstract concepts that can be confusing and divisive. This is true even for executives who are *supportive* of the concepts. Too often leaders find it difficult to frame these concepts in ways that inform their investment decisions. Stakeholder value requires a change in the mind-set of leaders and a disciplined approach to integrating it throughout the business. The article details how stakeholders – from employees to local communities and NGOs – are becoming a new, fast-growing source of business advantage.

This article offers a practical approach to building competitive advantage by identifying and acting on stakeholder-related business risks and opportunities. This disciplined approach, which integrates stakeholder considerations into core business strategy and operations, can help senior executives and line managers to create above-average returns. The authors, moreover, offer many excellent examples that illustrate how the competitive strategies of some of the world's largest businesses are changing as their leaders begin to take on a number of the world's most important social, environmental and economic issues as they work with stakeholder value.

The authors, experts in both the theory and the praxis of going-green, posit a new leadership vision and a disciplined approach to creating stakeholder value. The literature review included stakeholder thinking, strategic management, competitive advantage of corporate philanthropy, the learning organization and corporate social and environmental responsibility. There are many research areas that could now build on this, including the investigation of the development of new organizational leadership skills and competencies for the effective application of stakeholder value strategic decision-making in organizations.

The authors stress that the primary barrier to adopting a stakeholder perspective stems from the leader's mind-set, not from whether or not there is business value to be found. The goal is not only competing with industry rivals but also understanding and managing the changing expectations of an ever-growing and diverse set of stakeholders. The authors direct readers to Peter Senge's theory of mental models (1990). Laszlo et al. (2005, p. 70) add:

> Mind-set can be understood as the hidden set of beliefs about the individual, others and the world. Much like underlying operating systems in computers which allow only certain application software to run, our mind-sets dictate the range of possibilities we draw on to solve problems. . . Historically, the mind-set required to rise to the top of a large corporation has run counter to understanding, much less applying a stakeholder perspective in the process of value creation.

The authors speak from their experience when they state that courage, innovation and leadership can create competitive advantage by understanding the organization's key stakeholders' interests, anticipating societal expectations and using the insight, skills and relationships developed through this process to design new products and services, shape new markets, develop new business models and ultimately reshape the business context itself to one that supports the creation of truly sustainable value.

Reference

Senge, P.M. 1990. The fifth displine. *The Art and Practice of the Learning Organization*. New York: Currency Doubleday.

Lynes, J.K. and Andrachuk, M. 2008. Motivations for corporate social and environmental responsibility: A case study of Scandinavian Airlines. *Journal of International Management*, 14(4): 377–90.

The authors focus their research on the questions they lived with: 'Do we understand what drives a firm to be committed to social and environmental issues? Can this be unpacked into dynamic layers of internal, sector-specific and external influences?' In their study of the literature of motivations related to environmental as well as corporate social responsibility (CSER), they concluded 'that even now, when there are many studies that have provided descriptions of a firm's CSER motivations both within and across sectors (e.g. Bansal and Roth, 2000; Egri et al., 2004; Henriques and Sadorsky, 1996; Sharma, 2000), there is still a critical need to bring this literature together to address, in a systematic way, the interaction of these influences at the level of the firm'. This article helps us consider strategic options for CSER organizational and leadership development by helping to develop understanding of the reasons why corporations commit to CSER.

The definition of CSER has similarities to CSR, in that it refers to the commitment of firms to contribute to both social and environmental goals. The authors discover that common themes emerge from the literature, further defining CSER, including: regulatory compliance, voluntary initiatives, accountability, communication and transparency as well as institutionalization of environmental and social issues.

This study develops a model that illustrates the relationships between various influences on CSER: (1) how various external, sector-specific and internal influences for CSER are interpreted and then shaped into action at the level of the firm, and (2) exploring how this model applies to one firm, Scandinavian Airlines (SAS), by using an in-depth case study approach. Lynes and Andrachuk help unlock the figurative black box of SAS's motivations and expands the understanding of reasons why corporations are choosing (or not) to commit to CSER. If those reasons are known, they can be used to develop appropriate mechanisms to ensure that CSER is an important aspect of a company's decision-making system.

Their review of the research by A. Prakash (2000) revealed an inadequate understanding of the internal processes that lead a firm to adopt, or not adopt, environmental policies. Furthermore, they argue that an examination of intra-firm dynamics is required to supplement the existing literature on external pressures that firms face. Moreover, Lynes and Andrachuk's work adds to the literature in the international research related to CSER. Also, this is the first study to examine CSER in the airline industry.

This research offers a complex, but clear model-case-study approach to exploring the following questions: (1) What are the internal, sector-specific and the external factors that influence the interpretation of a firm's motivations and, ultimately, its level of commitment to CSER? (2) How do the motivations for social and environmental responsibility of a firm compare in terms of similarities and differences?

Citing Egri et al. (2004), the authors maintain that the application of CSER may be more effective in certain cultures. One of the strengths of this case study is that it provides further evidence that motivations cannot be looked at in isolation of sectoral and cultural contexts. Also, a catalyst, described as 'the lens through which a firm sees and interprets motivations' (p. 388) can have an important impact on a firm's level of commitment to CSER. Indicators that do not take into account the range of circumstances that influence corporate commitment towards both social and environmental responsibility risk failure.

The results section is structured around the model presented. The first half describes the four systems of influence for SAS, while the second half focuses on the motivations and catalysts that influence SAS's commitment to social and environmental responsibility.

In the end, this study and its conceptual model contributes to the existing literature by unpacking the layers of influences that affect SAS's motivations for both social and environmental responsibility and framing these in a way that allows deeper insight into the relationships between them. The study and model could be used as to base from which future studies can complement or compare the existing findings. Understanding influences on decision-making can determine the mechanisms needed to ensure continuous improvement of CSER.

References

Banasal, P. and Roth, K. 2000. Why companies go green: A model of ecological reponsiveness. *Academy of Management Journal*, **43**(4): 717–36.
Egri, C.P., Ralston, D.A., Milton, L., Naoumova, I., Palmer, I., Ramburuth, P., Wangenheim, F., Fu, P., Kuo, M.H., Ansari, M., Carranza, M.T.G., Riddle, L., Girson, I., Elenkov, D., Dabic, M., Butt, A., Srinivasan, N., Potocan, V.V., Furrer, O., Hallinger, P., Dalgic, T., Thanh, H.V., Richards, M. and Rossi, A.M. 2004. Managerial perpectives on corporate environmental and social responsibilities in 22 countries. Academy of Management Best Conference Paper 2004, pp. C1–C6.
Henriques, I. and Sadorsky, P. 1999. The relationship between environmental commitment and managerial perceptions of stakeholder performance. *Academy of Management Journal*, **42**(1): 87–99.
Prakash, A. 2000. *Greening the Firm: The Politics of Corporate Environmentalism.* Cambridge: Cambridge University Press.
Sharma, S. 2000. Managerial interpretations and organizational context as predictors of corporate choice of environmental strategy. *Academy of Management Journal*, **43**(4): 681–97.

Szekely, F. and Knirsch, M. 2005. Responsible leadership and corporate social responsibility: Metrics for sustainable performance. *European Management Journal*, **23(6): 628–47.**

This article provides managers with a practical guide to strategic planning and implementation of sustainable business initiatives. Twenty German businesses are researched. The article offers leaders an introduction to what role leadership plays in promoting sustainability in an organization. The extensive first half of the article is both a practical overview and how-to guide that includes sets of detailed checklists. This is an introductory guide for leaders who are in the process of engaging in a careful examination of internal and external factors that build a sustainable business. The top opportunities, barriers and challenges for sustainability initiatives, as well as a brief history of organizations working on sustainability in both Europe and Germany, are presented.

Although there are many companies that have initiated a variety of sustainable development initiatives meant to address the demands and expectations of society, there are still many managers who are not convinced of the validity of the claim that it contributes to business profitability. Szekely and Knirsch (2005) explain that most sustainable development initiatives have been developed in isolation of business activity and are not yet directly linked to business strategy. They add that one way to strengthen the link between the two is to measure the extent to which a company's performance increases as a result of implementing sustainable development initiatives. This paper articulates a need to establish clear, user-friendly methodologies and tools to measure the progress that companies are making toward sustainability.

The first half of the article sets the stage for the second half where the authors unveil the findings of their research that included a thorough examination of the best available metrics used by 20 major German businesses to measure their sustainability performance. Their examination of those businesses uncovered the various approaches that have been used to measure, monitor and assess a company's progress toward sustainability, including: sustainability surveys, sustainability metrics, sustainability indexes, performance indicators, award schemes, investor criteria, accountability, reporting, internal and external communication tools, benchmarking, accreditation processes, standards, codes, social screening services, screening systems and sustainability performance ranking.

Future research may be in methods of measuring and reporting of organizational sustainability initiatives. The authors conclude that none of the methods used by the 20 German businesses represented a clear universal tool that could be used by all industries or by all businesses within the same industry.

The analysis of the sustainability metrics of the sample businesses also shows a large discrepancy in what and how the companies measure and report concerning their sustainability performance. The reporting of sustainability practices varies from company to company, and, according to the authors, it is often difficult to understand and compare reporting methods.

Additional research could include: (1) identifying innovative external incentives; (2) studies on adoption of transformational internal management practices that turn businesses into sustainable institutions; and (3) current best practices of businesses that have both adopted the global Reporting Initiative (GRI) and are also participating in the Global Compact Initiative.

The authors note that most of the businesses they analyzed adopted the GRI's Sustainability Reporting Guidelines. The authors also found that most of the businesses in the study are participating in the United Nations' Global Compact Initiative. The authors comment on this firm initiative:

> In doing so, they feel they are adequately reporting the sustainable performance of their companies to society. The reality is that society expects much more from sustainability reporting. It is asking for greater transparency and easier access to information on the social and ecological impacts of companies. The adoption of the GRI guidelines represents a good start. However, the guidelines still need to be improved and refined. The Global Compact Initiative seems to be more of an exercise in improving the image of companies than an undertaking with strong and visionary leadership designed to promote the serious internal structural changes that companies require to become more sustainable. (Szekely and Knirsch, 2005, p. 645)

Since this research project was carried out, much has changed. The Global Compact and the GRI have developed. A current review of the literature related to both GRI and the UN Global Compact and their work with leaders and organizations would assist in formulating the needed next steps for research.

The GRI is a network-based organization that has pioneered the development of the world's most widely used sustainability reporting framework and is committed to its continuous improvement and application worldwide (http://www.globalreporting.org/Home).

Launched in July 2000, the United Nations Global Compact is a both a policy platform and a practical framework for companies that are committed to sustainability and responsible business practices. As a leadership initiative endorsed by chief executives, it seeks to align business operations and strategies everywhere with ten universally accepted principles in the areas of human rights, labor, environment and anti-corruption (http://www.unglobalcompact.org/).

REVIEWS BY DEAN HENNESSY

Del Río, P. 2009. The empirical analysis of the determinants for environmental technological change: A research agenda. *Ecological Economics*, **68(3): 861–78.**

This paper is a review of the literature on the determinants of environmental technological change. Environmental technological change refers to 'new or modified processes, techniques, practices, systems and products to avoid or reduce environmental harms' (Beise and Rennings, 2005, p. 6). Though environmental technologies can be grouped into several categories, the most commonly used distinction is between end-of-pipe (EOP) and cleaner technologies. Cleaner technology is considered superior because it cuts waste at the source. The author argues that the determinants of environmental technological change have not received much attention in the environmental/ecological economics literature. So, he attempts to identify a number of open questions in this context and to develop a framework for future analysis.

The paper argues that future analysis should address several issues at different levels: that is, regarding the conceptual framework, the thematic scope of the studies, some methodological issues and other aspects related to the environmental policy variable. An integrated conceptual framework that takes into account the interplay between relevant variables influencing environmental technological change (i.e., factors internal and external to the firm and characteristics of the environmental technologies) and all the stages of this process, with a greater emphasis on the invention stage, should be developed. Other aspects should then be tackled, including a focus on several themes (i.e., a greater attention to cross-sectoral technologies, the barriers to different types of environmental technologies, the international dimension of environmental technological change, and environmental technological change in small and medium-size enterprises), methodological issues (a combination of case studies and econometric modeling) and several issues related to the environmental policy variable.

The review of the literature is comprehensive. It deals not only with public policy issues, but also with firm-level behavior. In particular, incentives to either adopt environmentally friendly technology as inputs and develop and implement green technology in the production process or to produce outputs that have a positive environmental impact are critical in realizing the public agenda. Environmental innovation is not always top-down since, according to the so-called Porter Hypothesis, stricter environmental regulations are supposed to encourage environmental technologies that both reduce the environmental impact of production activities and the costs of complying with regulation.

Despite the relevance and importance of this topic to management in general, research on environmental technology and innovation has yet to be seriously taken up in the mainstream management journals. This represents an opportunity for management scholars, and this paper is helpful in identifying some key issues and fruitful avenues for future research relevant to management.

Reference

Beise, M. and Rennings, K. 2005. Lead markets for environmental innovations: A framework for innovation and environmental economics. *Ecological Economics*, 52(1): 5–17.

Jaffe, A.B., Newell, R.G. and Stavins, R.N. 2005. A tale of two market failures: Technology and environmental policy. *Ecological Economics*, 54(2–3): 164–74.

This is a concise policy-oriented paper dealing with how market failures associated with environmental pollution policy interact with market failures associated with the innovation and diffusion of new technologies. In this view, policy is related to regulating industry (e.g., targeting emissions), and technology innovations are related to firm-level incentives to develop new pollution control equipment, cleaner production methods, or new substitutes for environmentally harmful products. The authors argue that both theory and evidence suggest that the rate and direction of technological advance is influenced by market and regulatory incentives, and can be cost-effectively harnessed through the use of economic-incentive-based policy. They suggest that in the presence of weak or non-existent environmental policies, investments in the development and diffusion of new environmentally beneficial technologies are very likely to be less than would be socially desirable.

The authors also argue that these combined market failures provide a strong rationale for a portfolio of public policies that foster emissions reduction as well as the development and adoption of environmentally beneficial technology. Positive knowledge and adoption spillovers and information problems can further weaken innovation incentives. They argue that while difficult to implement, a long-term environmental technology policy suggests a strategy of experimentation with policy approaches and a systematic evaluation of their success.

The idea of a dual market failure is novel and interesting. It is certainly important to consider environmental policy as a complement to technology policy. In effect, they are both policy issues and so this is really about the 'optimal' mix of policy mechanisms (subject to short- and long-run objectives). Policies to reduce pollution have two effects – they have an immediate effect on pollution reduction and they also typically change the incentives that firms face regarding investing resources in developing new technology for the future. They are certainly right in arguing that this is made more complicated by the fact that these likely interact. (Though, it might also be thought of as a kind of two-level failure.) However, the conclusion that a 'portfolio of policies' is the solution is a bit of a cop-out. Portfolio options are often costly and policy prescriptions are always subject to budget constraints. Appropriate policy solutions are ones that take account of social benefits (relative effectiveness) for given levels of (social) costs. For my taste, specifying a model that clearly shows the relationships between variables would have been helpful in articulating the non-linearities and endogeneity, and so on, associated with the interaction between these two sets of policy mechanisms. Shifts in demand (due to changing tastes/preferences) might also be included in the equation. Nonetheless, this is still a useful overview of the key issues in an important policy debate.

Reinstaller, A. 2005. Policy entrepreneurship in the co-evolution of institutions, preferences, and technology: Comparing the diffusion of totally chlorine free pulp bleaching technologies in the US and Sweden. *Research Policy*, 34(9): 1366–84.

This paper presents detailed case studies on the transition to and diffusion of totally chlorine free (TCF) pulp bleaching methods in Sweden and the US. This change was sustained in the former, while it was almost absent in the latter. The author uses the concept of policy entrepreneurship to explain the social processes underlying sustainable technical change in the pulp and paper industry in the 1990s. Policy entrepreneurs identify social problems and develop a policy vision about what feasible solutions might exist. They set up pressure groups, organize social coalitions and initiate social bandwagons with the aim of triggering a public debate and gaining influence on the policy process. Reinstaller (2005) argues that the rise of TCF demand was related to the ability of policy entrepreneurs to link the pulp bleaching issue to already perceived environmental threats in Germany, while it failed to do so in the US because of a biased risk perception. In his view, such policy entrepreneurial actions are an effective means to change consumer behavior and affect technology choices by firms.

The second dominant theme of the paper is that of coevolution between technology, institutions and consumer preferences that took place in both countries. Reinstaller (2005) argues that differences in the two countries can be accounted for by viewing this as a complex process of the endogenous formation of preferences, the resulting market demand and technology choices by firms. The author concludes that transitions to sustainable paths in production and consumption may be supported by economic and social policy. Neither pure techno-economic nor market-based criteria determine the outcome. The author suggests that the role of policy should go beyond pure regulation, to include the dissemination of information, the support of policy entrepreneurship and involved interest groups.

This is a very interesting case of a 'dirty' industry that has transitioned to cleaner technology processes. It is made more interesting by the fact that the evolution and diffusion of cleaner technology in two different national settings differs. Some data are presented to establish differences in diffusion rates but thereafter, the paper relies on various accounts to create case histories. This is a strength and a weakness. It is a strength in the sense that it is a kind of appreciative theorizing that provides rich detail; it is a weakness in the sense that the link between particular events and the rate of adoption is not always clear. Also, while coevolution is the theoretical frame of reference, it appears that policy entrepreneurship is the prime mover – the mechanism by which change occurs. In this sense, it is not obvious why this is about coevolution since social entrepreneurship appears to be primarily exogenous. Still, this is a compelling case that adds to the critical social dimension of how environmental technologies diffuse.

REVIEWS BY LAURIE INGRAHAM

Tello, S.F. and Yoon, E. 2008. Examining drivers of sustainable innovation. *Journal of International Business Strategy*, **8(3): 164–9.**

This paper is a descriptive study of the relationships between a company's view on economic growth and environmental responsibility and the drivers that might encourage their response. The purpose is to explain the interaction between the company, the drivers and the stakeholder groups. Three viewpoints are examined: the trade-off view, the synergy view and the social responsibility view.

In the trade-off view, there is a struggle between a company's bottom line and economic growth and environmental concerns. The drivers that impact the balance of this struggle are government regulation and social activism. Both apply pressure on enterprises to spend additional resources for environmental issues.

The synergy view suggests that investing in the environment can create new industries and thus foster new economic growth. Customer demand for sustainable products and advances in sustainable technologies spur companies to move towards a more synergistic viewpoint. This involves educating the consumer on the impacts of specific industries on the environment and the importance of resource conservation. With an educated public, they will be more apt to purchase products from companies invested in the environment or new sustainable products and this will cause economic growth. The development of new clean technologies supports the more efficient use of natural resources (Costanza et al., 2000) and provides solutions to many global concerns (climate change, scarcity of resources, etc.).

Taking social responsibility for the environment is the third viewpoint discussed (CSR) and is based on stakeholder theory. Rather than being focused on only the bottom line, this view sees the corporation as a social institution that must consider the interests of all of the groups that it impacts (Shaw, 2007). The drivers that encourage this view are corporate initiatives for sustainable innovation and cooperative operation of sustainable supply chain partnerships.

The contribution of this paper is the discussion concerning the drivers that influence a company's viewpoint and decision-making process. As the authors mentioned, this theoretical framework represents initial steps towards a more robust research paper. Perhaps, assessing the relationships amongst the variables – views, drivers, responses and strategies – using correlations would make the research more complete. The concluding table would have been more compelling had it been accompanied by a more comprehensive literature view of the three viewpoints and the drivers earlier on in the paper. Also, more discussion about possible business strategies might create a more inclusive picture of how the different areas interact with each other.

References
Costanza, R., Daly, H., Folke, C. and Hawken, P. 2000. Managing our environmental portfolio. *Bioscience*, **50**(2): 149–55.
Shaw, W.H. 2007. *Business Ethics* (6th edn). Belmont, CA: Thompson Wadsworth.

Thomson, D. and Khare, A. 2008. Carbon capture and storage (CCS) deployment – can Canada capitalize on experience? *Journal of Technology Management and Innovation*, **3(4): 111–18.**

The current relevance of carbon capture and storage (CCS) makes it an interesting read and proposes some suitable questions for the nation of Canada, while providing helpful updates for international communities seeking information about this new technology. The article represents a general overview of the definition of CCS and suggests Canada as a potential world leader in the future technology of this developing industry.

The authors point out that capturing carbon will only be a part of a five-strategy solution in order to prevent the escalation of GHG (greenhouse gas) emissions in the next 50 years (Socolow and Greenblatt, 2008). They speculate that Canada is in a good position to promote this technology for several reasons: (1) the geological formations in the Western Canadian Sedimentary Basin (WCSB) have 'cap' rock to act as a barrier to GHG movement (Griffiths et al., 2005), (2) Canada has industries with related experience (gas processing companies) and (3) it has a current working pilot project (EnCana's Weyburn).

Using descriptions and definitions as the focus of the research, the paper lacks any research methodology; it uses articles from websites rather than from academic journals. Since the topic is so new, there may be few available academic research articles. However, I was disappointed that current scholars/geoengineers in the area of CCS were ignored such as David Keith (Keith et al., 2006) and other scientists (Keller et al., 2003) who could offer a more technical and research-based viewpoint.

As an introduction to the definition of CCS and as a description of the process, this paper could be a useful tool for gaining a basic knowledge of the science. It also provides a good overview of the current global projects that exist so that individuals seeking more information could look further. However, as far as filling a gap in the research, there are methodological research papers available that can support the argument for Canada as a leader in CCS technology. Perhaps, a more thorough literature review would create a useful exploratory research paper for academics seeking information on this topic.

References

Griffiths, M., Cobb, P. and Marr-Laing, T. 2005. Carbon capture and storage: An arrow in the quiver or a silver bullet to combat climate change? A Canadian primer. Available at: http://www.pembina.org/pub/584; accessed 17 June 2010.

Keith, D.W., Ha-Duong, M. and Stolaroff, J.K. 2006. Climate strategy with CO_2 capture from the air. *Climatic Change*, **74**(1–3): 17–45.

Keller, K., Yand, Z. and Hall, M. 2003. Carbon dioxide sequestration: When and how much? Princeton University, Center for Economic Policy Studies. Climate Change Working Paper No.108.

Socolow, R. and Greenblatt, J. 2008. Solving the climate problem: Technologies available to curb CO_2 emissions. *Environment*, **46**(10): 8–19.

Van Alphen, K., Van Ruijven, J., Kasa, S., Hekkert, M. and Turkenburg, W. 2009. The performance of the Norwegian carbon dioxide, capture and storage innovation system. *Energy Policy*, 37(2): 43–55.

Policy implementation is a challenging process for most innovative technologies and CCS (carbon capture and storage) poses some interesting questions for policy-makers of the future in this industry. The Norwegian technology system for CCS is respected worldwide, not only for being one of the originators of the 'know-how', but also for creating a model for policy-making and government support necessary for its success.

The authors provide an analysis of the CCS technology in Denmark to discover what future policy issues need to be addressed in order to continue Norway's international leadership in this area. A technological innovation system (TIS) (Jacobsson and Bergek, 2004; Foxon et al., 2005) analyzes the network of actors interacting in a technological area and links it with socio-technological change. A TIS has three main components: actors, institutions and their relationship networks. This framework of innovation system functions to describe the evolution of the Norwegian CCS system and evaluate its performance.

Seven functions that were used in previous research (Hekkert et al., 2007; Bergek et al., 2008) are used to assess the dynamics of this CCS innovation system in order to arrive at policy recommendations. The theoretical portion of the paper explains in detail each of the functions and how they can be applied to innovative technologies; this helps the reader make the connection to Denmark's CCS technology analysis later in the paper.

Three types of data collection were used: (1) review of scientific and gray literature (newspaper articles, etc.), (2) 20 interviews with main stakeholders in development, and (3) a narrative of the appearance and evolution of Norway's CCS innovation system. However, the methodology section is difficult to find and is woven within the theoretical framework. It would be helpful if there had been a section to illustrate how they carried out the research. Perhaps, describing in more detail how the research evolved (i.e., how were the interviews conducted and what research tools were used to analyze the data) would build a better connection to the results and allow future researchers to follow their methodology for studies of other countries (as suggested in their final comments). Also, the figures were interesting, but could have been more meticulous in their presentation.

The historical description of the CCS industry and its evolution in Denmark was valuable and will be useful for future research in this area. Also, the framework of the seven functions of CCS clearly represented the development, diffusion and use of the new technology; the presentation was effective and impactful.

The links between the seven function areas of analyses and policy recommendations for Denmark were plausible and informative. Conclusions include the imposition of a carbon tax; it's critical for encouraging entrepreneurs and private industry to devote the human resources and financial incentives to R&D for CCS technology. The government must also demonstrate early commitment to the technology to ensure success. At a critical time, CCS technology will advance or be deterred depending on who is the head of the national government.

Overall, this paper fills a knowledge gap and is a very complete account of what a country must do to develop an innovative technology plan for CCS. It contributes to future research by inviting other countries who are interested in CCS to discover their weaknesses and strengths in pursuing these projects. To make this innovative technology viable and long-lasting, relationships between industry, government, academic institutions and NGOs are necessary – partnerships and cooperation are vital.

References

Bergek, A., Jacobsson, S., Carlsson, B., Lindmark, S. and Rickne, A. 2008. Analyzing the functional dynamics of techological innovation systems: A scheme of analysis. *Research Policy*, **37**(3): 407–29.

Foxon, T., Gross, R., Chase, A., Howes, J., Arnall, A. and Anderson, D. 2005. UK innovation systems for new and renewable energy technologies: Drivers, barriers and systems failures. *Energy Policy*, **33**(16): 2123–37.

Hekkert, M., Suurs, R., Negro, S., Kuhlmann, S. and Smits, R. 2007. Functions of innovation systems: A new approach for analysing technological change. *Technological Forecasting and Social Change*, **74**(4): 413–32.

Jacobsson, S. and Bergek, A. (2004). Transforming the energy sector: the evolution of technological systems in renewable energy technology. *Industrial and Corporate Change*, **13**(5): 815–49.

REVIEWS BY OLGA HAWN

Horbach, J.J. 2008. Determinants of environmental innovation: New evidence from German panel data sources. *Research Policy*, **37(1): 163–73.**

Relying on two new German datasets, this exploratory empirical paper tests all of the existing environmental innovation theories that answer the following question: What is the driving force of environmental innovation? Is it 'new or modified processes, techniques, systems and products to avoid or reduce environmental damage' (Kemp et al., 2001)? The theories include the supply side, the demand side and institutional and political influences perspectives. Broadly, it concludes that all of them hold. Specifically, innovation breeds innovation, an increase in the expected future demand triggers environmental innovation and finally, environmental regulation, environmental management tools and general organizational changes and improvements help to reduce the information deficits about cost-saving potentials that encourage environmental innovation.

Thus, it seems that the theoretical contribution of this paper is quite limited: it is not developing a new theory or building on an existing one – it is just testing the previous literature with a new dataset. In fact, the only originality of this paper lies in the novelty of the datasets – dynamic (panel) data. However, there are limitations to it. First, the datasets were not collected with the objective of exploring environmental innovation, thus missing variables may be causing bias in the analyses (e.g., it is not possible to address endogeneity or reverse causality problems due to the lack of data). Second, there are problems with the full identification of firms implementing environmental innovation in the survey since not all of the participants in the initial year responded to the questionnaire in the following year. Finally, more integration of the two datasets and results is warranted: since the primary goal of this paper is to explore, it could have been much stronger had it set up 'a horse race' between the existing theories in an attempt to discover which one of them best answers the question (e.g., in absolute value).

As for the measures, some of them could have been improved, especially had the paper used other sources of data rather than relying on self-reported information from the firms. For example, the measure of 'demand' constitutes 'turnover expectations' but actual turnover may significantly differ from the expected; the paper seems to overlook this point. Another problem is the construction of a measure for 'environmental regulation'. 'Environmental regulation' in the first dataset is proxied by 'subsidies' that do not measure regulation – rather, they provide direct incentives for environmental innovation. The second dataset proxies for 'regulation' with a direct question in the survey, 'is fulfillment of regulations and standards a highly important motive of innovation?' (Horbach, 2008, p. 171) (it contains an inherent bias of directing the respondent to the right answer). Regulation could have been captured in a natural experiment with a change in policy, for example, new legislation, signing the Kyoto Protocol and imposing its standards on firms, starting the carbon trade by selling and buying credits. Overall, a more precise study could have better addressed this question. For example, an event study following a change in policy or a study situated in a specific industry that reacts (or does not react) to a specific environmental regulation would have been a better context for testing whether environmental regulation motivates environmental innovation or not.

Nevertheless, the analysis is well done and the findings do not falsify the contention that the improvement of the technological capabilities by R&D ('knowledge capital'), the expected demand for new (environmentally friendly) products, environmental regulation, environmental management tools and general organizational changes (Porter Hypothesis) support environmental innovation in the future. However, this paper is a good example of what not to do in a future study: do not use two datasets together; instead, maintain focus and be precise, seek novel answers to the research question, review literature from other fields to add a fresh perspective, build a clearly explained theory and logic for the hypotheses, triangulate with data sources and use appropriate measures.

Reference

Kemp, R., Arundel, A. and Smith, K. 2001. Survey indicators for environmental innovation. Paper presented to conference on Towards Environmental Innovation Systems in Garmisch – Partenkirchen.

Larson, A.L. 2000. Sustainable innovation through an entrepreneurship lens. *Business Strategy and the Environment*, 9(5): 304–17.

In this paper, Larson (2000) overviews the entrepreneurship literature and applies it to a case study of an innovation- and sustainability-based enterprise. She argues that entrepreneurship literature is relevant for studying sustainability because the latter is a source of change in society and the former can help explain how and why it takes place. It is not a novel idea in my mind (entrepreneurship literature can and has been applied to various fields of research); however, what Larson does well in this article is demonstrate with a case how 'the concepts of opportunity, innovation and future products and processes that unfold at the nexus of the opportunity and the entrepreneur' (p. 308) – the core of entrepreneurship – can apply to a sustainable innovation. Additionally, through the case study of Walden Paddlers, Larson (2000) answers the following research questions: Can innovative environmental management and sustainability occur in *new* firms? More specifically, how do smaller firms engaged in innovative environmental practices achieve *success*? Thus, this structure of the paper makes it a truly unique piece, theoretically converging with the resource-based view while contrary to the public policy view and voluntary standards perspective of sustainable innovation.

By shifting focus to innovation and smaller firms, Larson (2000) fills a gap in research about whether and how firms can achieve innovative environmental management and sustainability at the same time. Moreover, the paper shows how new firms engaged in innovative environmental practices can achieve success: by exploiting market inefficiencies, creating 'future' products and engaging partners and turning them around. Only with a case study could one answer such questions and find the conditions under which this will be possible. Thus, Walden Paddlers, as a case of Schumpeterian innovation, included the following elements: (1) economic opportunity in the growing market for inexpensive recreational kayaks and the abundant supply of relatively inexpensive recyclable plastics; (2) 'fit' between the entrepreneur and the opportunity in that Paul Farrow had environmental knowledge and personal values that motivated the start-up; (3) the experience and financial and analytic skills of the entrepreneur; (4) the attention to detail, for example, the mission statement; (5) the alternative mode of organization – the virtual corporation or network to avoid overhead expenses; (6) continuous learning and adaptability, for example, the first time they did not manage to produce a kayak from 100 percent recycled plastic, persistency helped create one later.

The research design section is the only part that raises doubts. First, I disagree with the statement that the ethnographic information can only be gathered though interviews. Ethnography primarily involves observations, thus, interviews are just one way to deepen them, but not the only means to collect such data. Second, it is not clear whether the author is arguing in favor of or against case studies by saying that 'case studies have obvious limits in terms of generalizability, but can be used in conjunction with other research results to suggest patterns' (p. 308). On the whole, the fit between the research design and the purpose of the paper was not well considered: the author claims that with this case she intends to develop a theory but the introduction suggests that the purpose of the paper is to apply entrepreneurship literature to sustainable innovation.

Overall, I liked the case, but as usual the main criticism is derived from limitations of generalizability and representativeness (one success story does not imply that every enterprise, even given the same circumstances, will survive in the nearest future). The other criticism is in regards to the implementation: if the case work was done correctly, interviews with the people in the network (in addition to the entrepreneur) would have been included in the research design; however, the perspective provided in this study is limited by the one-sided argument of the main actor. As the author mentioned briefly, ethnographic data could have solved this problem but I guess in the network form of organization with access to only one key informer – the entrepreneur – this could have posed an additional challenge for the researcher. Thus, this paper provides a good but limited view of how entrepreneurship literature can be applied to innovative environmental management and sustainability.

Wagner, M. 2007. On the relationship between environmental management, environmental innovation and patenting: Evidence from German manufacturing firms. *Research Policy*, 36(10): 1587–602.

This paper can be divided into two parts: exploratory (identifying environmental innovations from patent data) and explanatory (finding alternative explanations outside the available theory base). It broadly answers the following research question: what is the relationship between environmental innovations, environmental management and patenting? In particular, it identifies how environmental management systems (EMS) and the interaction with environmentally concerned stakeholders are associated with the probability of firms pursuing innovation in general, and specifically, environmental innovation. It finds that the level of EMS implementation is what matters, not the signal from certification that takes place (or does not take place) after implementation.

   Three main contributions are made. First, this paper is a rare study using panel data so it can resolve the issue of reverse causality. Second, it discusses in fine detail all potential biases and most critical empirical issues such as, for example, endogeneity and, more importantly, how to correctly identify environmental innovation through panel data (without total reliance on the self-reported survey measures). Finally, this article truly serves its purpose as an explanatory-exploratory paper by providing an extensive list of potential causes for the findings and providing strong arguments in support of its conclusions. For example, Wagner (2007) finds that only 1.4 percent of all patents in the data are environmentally related. The four explanations given for this result include (1) other ways of IP protection such as secrecy, lead time or defensive publishing, (2) different types of financing, for example, public funding may require such innovations to be released to the public, (3) inconsistencies in the sample (only a small number of firms developed, produced or sold environmentally related technology as a part of their core business), and (4) the nature of environmental innovation (it could be so small that patenting is not feasible). The main conclusion from this exploration is that patents cannot be used to construct a measure of environmental innovation.

It is a very well-crafted paper. It addresses all potential critiques but its main weakness is that it does not provide a well-developed logic for its propositions. For example, the first proposition is built on a single premise that previous literature identified a link between EMS and innovative activity or firm reputation. There is no discussion about the levels of EMS implementation or propensity and/or activity levels for environmental process or product innovation. The author simply states that there *may be* an effect without listing any reasons for it; how the analysis will parse out the differences in the levels of implementation or how the dependent variable will be operationalized, however, is not explained. In an attempt to provide some reasoning for the propositions, right after stating them, Wagner (2007) mentions several theories like neo-institutional, stakeholder or resource-based views, but they are only applied to explain EMS as a signal, not to develop a theory that is tested in the paper.

The second set of propositions has similar problems: the author states that there *may be* a link between cooperative activities amongst environmentally oriented or neutral partners for environmental innovation and patenting activity. However, the distinction amongst the partners or the reasons why there would be any link (and if any, in what direction?) have not been discussed. Finally, since the paper uses propositions instead of hypotheses, the interpretation of the results is discretionary. For example, propositions 1, 3 and 5 can be supported to some extent but can also be rejected if more stringent conditions were to be added. For the reasons discussed, the article is only a modest start to addressing the empirical issues in research on environmental innovation using panel data.

6 Academic theory*
Dan V. Caprar, Jijun Gao, Elvira Haezendonck, Jonatan Pinkse and Svenja Tams

OVERVIEW BY DAN V. CAPRAR

The objective of the group was to identify which academic theories have been used in sustainability management literature and what might have motivated their use. We also aimed at exploring whether certain theories are more useful than others, and to what extent new or different theories are needed. The final goal of such exploration was to suggest future paths with regard to theorizing in this field.

While our review of the literature has not been exhaustive, we identified a range of theories that are currently used (of course, just like the article base, the list is not exhaustive – a more detailed review is needed, especially in order to determine prevalence of some theories over others). Based on our selective review, we could group theories employed in the sustainability literature into two categories: (1) firm-level explanations: for example, resource-based view (RBV), institutional theory, transaction costs, stakeholder theory/perspective, resource dependency; (2) individual-level explanations: for example, symbolic/political perspectives, constructive developmental individual differences.

It appears that no unique theory for green management has been formulated yet; however, a unique (or unified) theory may not be needed. Currently, several existing theories are used without any major adaptations to the field. There is an opportunity to further develop these theories using insights from sustainability; it appears that in general (just like in other fields, perhaps), there is more acceptance for integrating approaches and building on the existing theories, rather than challenging them with confrontational ideas. A natural question that sprung from these observations was what is (or should be) theory in general, and how such principles of 'good theory' would apply to this field.

A feature of the theory in this field is that it takes on a normative/prescriptive approach: most academics working on these topics strongly believe in the importance and value of sustainability. While this might be

---

* Facilitator: Dan V. Caprar.

a positive, desirable bias from a social impact perspective, from a scientific rigor point of view we must wonder to what extent, and how, this bias might influence our research agenda. We more or less agreed that theory is descriptive, explanatory and/or predictive in terms of its objectives, but we all agreed that theory is in essence about understanding. With that in mind, we formulated as possible paths for the future the acknowledgement and exploration of contradictions in sustainability theorizing, as this might lead to insights about what is unique about this field, how different theories might concur in explaining contradictions, along with – we believe – contrasting and confronting existing theories, when needed. Exploring cross-levels of analysis seems to be necessary; what remains debatable is to what extent a new, distinctive theory is possible, or even needed – for sure a rich and important area of future investigation.

REVIEWS BY JIJUN GAO

Hoffman, A.J. and Ocasio, W. 2001. Not all events are attended equally: Toward a middle-range theory of industry attention to external events. *Organization Science*, **12(4): 414–34.**

Past organizational research on critical events has focused on the sense-making processes, and little work has been done to investigate why some events become critical while others pass unnoticed. Existing theory on public attention focuses on competition for attention among broad social problems but does not pay attention to specific events. Drawing upon organizational theories on attention and identity, this paper fills the gap by answering two key questions: (1) What explains whether and when some events receive public attention within an industry, while others are ignored? (2) When and why do certain events attain high and sustained levels of industry attention? The concept of industry-level attention highlights 'how industry participants, in their communications and inter-actions with other industry participants, selectively focus their attention on a limited set of issues, situations and activities that represent potential problems or opportunities for the industry' (Hoffman and Ocasio, 2001, p. 415).

The research design involves a paired case comparison of media cover-age of eight environment-related events affecting the US chemical industry, spanning 35 years from 1960 to 1995. Recognizing that public attention is situated within particular channels of communication, the authors choose the trade journal, *Chemical Week*, as the primary information source for industry attention. Two newspapers, the *New York Times* and the *Wall Street Journal*, are chosen to represent externally situated perceptions of relevant events.

Using an analytical process that combines induction with deduction, this study proposes a set of hypotheses inferred from the case observations. A final model is developed that provides a coherent theoretical explanation of how the industry structures attention to non-routine occurrences. The key inference is: an event is more likely to receive industry-level attention when the outsiders hold the industry accountable for the event (H1); when the insiders are concerned with threatened industry image because of the event (H2); and when the appropriate social structures of attention are in place, including the congruence of the rules of the game with potential industry accountability for the event (H3), the high status of the players involved or affected by the event (H4) and the significant consequences of the event on the core technology of industry members (H5). Further, an event may become a critical issue with sustained industry attention when there is contestation with outsiders' attribution of accountability for the event and its enactment, and internal challenges to the industry's identity (H6).

The implications of this study to the theory development in the area of sustainability are threefold. First, given the long-term nature of sustainability phenomena, a historical or longitudinal approach may be needed in order to discover underlying patterns of evolution. A simple cross-sectional analysis may risk presenting a spurious relationship. Second, an industry level of analysis may allow us to disclose something unique that we might not be able to uncover with an organizational level of analysis. This is especially important considering the challenge of collecting organizational-level data and the suspect 'fact' that many firms are simply clustered in the middle in terms of social and environmental practices, resulting in little variation among them, which does not lend itself well to variance-based methods such as regression. Third, a focus on social events as they relate to institutional change provides a valuable opportunity to examine the recursive processes of institutional–organizational co-evolution. It also highlights the fact that the sustainability issues are essentially part of an institutional war.

Lewis, M.W. 2000. Exploring paradox: Toward a more comprehensive guide. *Academy of Management Review*, 25(4): 760–76.

Having an interest in organizational complexity and ambiguity, Lewis develops a framework that facilitates exploration of paradox in organizations. A paradox is when there occurs 'contradictory yet interrelated elements – elements that seem logical in isolation but absurd and irrational when appearing simultaneously' (Lewis, 2000, p.760). Paradoxes are socially constructed when people frequently simplify reality into polarized either/or distinctions in order to make sense of an increasingly intricate and ever-changing world. Such perceptual distinctions become objectified over time and cause tension when brought into proximity. Some examples of paradoxical tensions in organization studies include quality/cost, differentiation/integration, stability/change and autonomy/dependence.

The framework of this paper clarifies the nature of paradoxical tensions, reinforcing cycles involving different forms of paralyzing defense, and paradox management that taps the potential insights and power of paradox toward creative change. To illustrate the framework in use, the author reviews organization studies exploring paradoxes, and categorizes them into three groups: paradox of learning (tension between old and new), paradox of organizing (tension between control and flexibility) and paradox of belonging (tension between self and other).

Based on the reviewed exemplars, the author also outlines strategies for identifying paradoxes (such as narrative, psychodynamic and multi-paradigm approaches), and representing paradoxes (such as conceptualizing, mapping and theorizing).

Although this paper is not focused on sustainability phenomena, it points to a valuable perspective that may prove to be fruitful in future sustainability research. First, one thing very unique about sustainability issues is that they typically involve tension or contradiction of some sort, such as responsibility/costs, legitimacy/efficiency, social considerations/economic calculations, as well as society/business in general. Many tensions and polarities, socially constructed under a traditional business paradigm, obscure the interrelatedness and simultaneity of the contradictions; yet such simultaneity is at the core of business sustainability. It is thus important for scholars in this field to explore the paradoxes and address important questions such as what reinforcing cycles are at play, and how actors may manage paradoxes to foster change and develop accommodating mechanisms. Second, exploring paradoxes may offer frame-breaking experiences that move beyond the over-simplication and over-rationalization of complex phenomena. Third, qualitative approaches and even an interpretivist lens may be valuable to fully unveil the intricacy and complexity of individuals, group and organizations around sustainability commitment.

King, A. 2007. Cooperation between corporations and environmental groups: A transaction cost perspective. *Academy of Management Review*, 32(3): 889–900.

From a transaction cost perspective, this paper examines how corporations and environmental stakeholders organize cooperative efforts in a world of high transaction costs. A set of hypotheses are proposed based on prominent empirical examples. The analyses provide explanations for three main issues around the cooperation: (1) how a win-win technology (i.e., both environmentally and financially superior production option) may be co-developed that solves the hold-up problem for corporations and stakeholders, as a result of stakeholder investment in the technology; (2) how ex post transaction costs may be reduced by selecting honest and credible partners and developing long-term relations that prevent reneging; (3) how conflicts of interest amongst stakeholder roles can be reduced by separating the stakeholder's corporate engagement and auditing activities. The paper also emphasizes that any theory about the role of corporations as agents for positive social change should consider the relationship between corporations and stakeholders, particularly how barriers to mutually beneficial exchange may be reduced through certain ways of structuring the relations.

Despite its negative and highly economic assumptions on the nature of corporations and stakeholders because of the theory being used, this paper offers important insights to theory building in business sustainability research. First, analysis on broad sustainability issues and stakeholder relations, in particular, asks for a transaction cost perspective, given the reality that both firms and stakeholders face significant transaction costs such as negotiating, monitoring and enforcement, when pushing for their own benefits. At the same time, this field represents a promising area for extending transaction costs theory because it is unique in the sense that firms and stakeholders are barred from creating a hierarchy in response to high transaction costs. In other words, the conventional 'make or buy' decision does not apply here; rather, a certain hybrid governance mechanism for cooperation has to be created.

Second, even though the terms such as 'pressure' or 'response' are frequently used in discussing corporate social and environmental practices, we might need to acknowledge that cooperation, rather than tension, coercion and struggle, is the best solution to advancing a sustainable model of business. Embracing a paradigm of cooperation means that we should pay more attention to the mechanisms of win–win solutions, instead of focusing on blaming and constraining firms. Third, since different nations and economies have dramatically different patterns of firm–stakeholder relations as well as transaction costs structure means that it would be fruitful to investigate the cooperation in an international context.

REVIEWS BY ELVIRA HAEZENDONCK

Hart, S.L. 1995. A natural-resource-based view of the firm. *Academy of Management Review*, **20(4): 969–1014.**

The current RBV of corporate environmental strategy has its roots in Hart's (1995) seminal article. In fact, he was the first to have provided a coherent theoretical model linking corporate environmental strategy choices; bundles of investments, in particular, resource domains; the subsequent creation of firm-specific environmental capabilities; and, ultimately, competitive advantage.

Hart (1995) developed a typology of corporate environmental strategy that distinguishes among four environmental strategy choices, namely: pollution control, pollution prevention, product stewardship and sustainable development. Each environmental strategy is characterized by specific sets of valuable and rare resources, which are difficult to substitute or imitate (Barney, 1991; Hart, 1995). In contrast to other well-known typologies in this sphere (e.g., Roome, 1992 and Azzone and Bertele, 1994), Hart's typology emphasizes the interactions among the various environmental strategy stages and the process to move from one stage to the next.

Specifically, to the extent that pollution control strategies are expensive and non-productive, whereas prevention strategies may lead to a cost advantage through increased productivity and efficiency, some firms choose to improve their financial bottom line by investing in pollution prevention strategies. Subsequently, a firm engaged in pollution prevention could foray into product stewardship, gaining benefits from product differentiation, and finally into sustainable development, leading in the best case to a more secure future competitive position. Pollution prevention, product stewardship and sustainable development are 'proactive' corporate environmental strategies since they involve environmental investments by the firm beyond those required by regulation. However, Hart's main point is that each step towards higher proactivity is contingent upon earlier steps, which have a cumulative effect and are embedded in a particular path dependent trajectory. For example, Hart discusses how the firm's investments in pollution prevention may contribute to success in product stewardship, and how investments in both pollution prevention and product stewardship may be instrumental to the success of a sustainable development strategy. The interesting question is then why some firms choose to engage themselves on this environmental strategy path, whereas others do not. As Hart says 'what is it that predisposes some firms to make the bold move ahead of others?' (p. 1008). The current environmental RBV literature's answer is that this is at least in part due to the firm's environmental investments in a series of interrelated resource domains (Verbeke et al., 2006).

A weakness in Hart's work is his narrow focus: this environmental RBV approach should be placed in the broader organizational context that takes into account parameters such as ecocentric leadership and related values as the drivers of environmental investments. In Verbeke et al. (2006), it is argued that the RBV on corporate environmental strategy, guided by Hart's (1995) insights, can be extended in two significant ways. First, the direct and specific connections between investments (resource domains), firm-specific capabilities and competitive advantage should be made more explicit. Second, investment decisions in Hart-type resource domains should be explained by multiple parameters in the wider organizational context, a point well understood in the broader RBV strategy literature. An integrative RBV model of corporate environmental strategy resulted in Verbeke et al. from the above extensions of Hart's work.

Further research was undertaken by Verbeke et al. (2006) and more recently in an empirical paper of Sellers and Verbeke (2009); they have built on Hart and argued that investments in specific resource domains, not environmental strategy per se, ultimately determine environmental performance.

References

Azzone, G. and Bertele, U. 1994. Exploiting green strategies for competitive advantage. *Long Range Planning*, **27**(6): 69–81.
Barney, J. 1991. Firm resources and sustained competitive advantage. *Journal of Management*, **17**(1): 99–120.
Roome, N. 1992. Developing environmental management strategies. *Business Strategy and the Environment*, **1**(1): 11–24.
Sellers, M. and Verbeke, A. 2009. Greening and competitive advantage: An empirical analysis of the Canadian oil and gas industry. Unpublished doctoral dissertation, University of Calgary, Calgary.
Verbeke, A., Bowen, F. and Sellers, M. 2006. Corporate environmental strategy: Extending the natural-resource-based view of the firm. Best Paper Proceedings Annual Meeting of the Academy of Management, Atlanta.

Ilinitch, A.Y. and Schaltegger, S.C. 1995. Developing a green business portfolio. *Long Range Planning*, **28(2): 29–38.**

Ilinitch and Schaltegger (1995) have advocated the use of an ecologically oriented portfolio analysis, integrating environmental elements into traditional portfolio analysis in order to address emerging strategic environmental issues. Their 'green business portfolio' matrix quantifies the environmental impact of business activities and compares it with the economic performance of these businesses, the latter being based upon conventional indicators, that is, relative market share and relative growth rate. The economic performance dimensions are the same as those used in the Boston Consulting Group (BCG) matrix and result in the familiar matrix with four quadrants. Introducing an environmental impact dimension leads to the development of a three-dimensional matrix (3D matrix). Ilinitch and Schaltegger (1995) have estimated the environmental effect by using 'pollution units' or the discharges of toxic substances in air, land and water. The horizontal plane represents the performance dimensions. The vertical axis represents the environmental impact. The higher the position on the vertical axis, the 'cleaner' the business can be considered in relative terms. The size of the circles can represent the size of the firm in relative environmental or economic terms (Ilinitch and Schaltegger, 1995).

The optimal position in the ecologically oriented product portfolio analysis of Ilinitch and Schaltegger (1995) is the 'green star' that combines high economic performance with low environmental harm. A 'dirty dog' position is not a desirable position in the matrix: this position reflects products or businesses that cause substantial environmental harm without contributing significant economic benefits in terms of market share or growth rate. In addition to these two extreme cells, a number of 'middle positions' exist, such as a 'dirty cash cow', a 'green dog' or a 'green question mark'. A 'dirty cash cow' reflects a high market share in dirty technologies. A 'green dog' position suggests a combination of a weak economic performance within an environmentally attractive business.

When developing their 3D matrix including an environmental dimension, Ilinitch and Schaltegger (1995) also identified three important conditions for its proper use. First, it is important to analyze firms on a relative basis. Through benchmarking, environmentally proactive companies can be identified. Second, the analysis should be dynamic (or at least comparatively static) in order to allow the observation of shifts in environmental performance over time. Third, in addition to the absolute performance, the relative performance through a correction for size should also be considered, as large firms may be more polluting than smaller ones in absolute terms, yet more environmentally friendly, when taking into account their turnover, than smaller companies.

The strength of this contribution was undoubtedly the practitioners'-oriented introduction of a visual way of presenting green benchmarking. It interestingly combines insights from the positioning school with environmental strategy. It offers a useful tool for practitioners that is at the same time very visual and easy to use in Microsoft Excel. Moreover, it links theory with clear policy- and strategy-oriented results.

Some weaknesses are found in the paper. Fully harmonized datasets on green performance were missing and there was a lack of thorough understanding of performance evaluation (third-dimension values should be available and relevant for the green performance of the industry considered). Additionally, I found a lack of theoretical support and integration of other research insights on performance.

Within the constraints of the portfolio application suggested in this paper and by incorporating the current research (for example, indicators of green performance) the revitalization of an iconic framework such as the BCG matrix could well serve managers and firms today for environmental strategy. Or, as Cummings and Daellenbach (2009, p.258) suggested, 'Perhaps something valuable has been lost. How might we retrieve it?' Cummings and Daellenbach (2009) strongly believe in a return to knowledge and best practices of recent decades. 'Back to the future', they call it.

Reference
Cummings, S. and Daellenbach, U. 2009. A guide to the future of strategy? The history of long range planning. *Long Range Planning*, **42**(2): 234–63.

Rugman A.M. and Verbeke, A. 1998. Corporate strategies and environmental regulations: An organizing framework. *Strategic Management Journal*, **19(4): 363–75.**

Rugman and Verbeke (1998) clarify the recent environmental strategy literature up to 1998. They develop several charts in their article, all very valuable conceptual insights to the structuring of the literature and are useful to every scholar active or interested in the domain of environmental strategy.

The article tackles research questions that were important at the time. During the 1990s, for example, the environmental management literature was dominated by the question of whether the economic and environmental performance of companies was positively or negatively related. They also tried to understand and explain why companies do or do not make green investments, a stream of literature that is still studied today. Another issue was the impact of environmental regulation on the competitive position of countries and companies (MNEs). Rugman and Verbeke's (1998) point was that regulations are a trigger for proactive rather than reactive responses.

The authors use a micro-perspective (i.e., from the viewpoint of the company or its managers) to discuss their research questions. This level is studied in most environmental management articles because green investments are initiated by the company, its drivers and facilitators. The macro-level is also discussed in regards to the role of environmental regulations on the competitive position of countries (macro-level) and the resulting consequences for MNEs (micro-level). The meso-level, in-between, is not discussed. It was not an important level of study at the time and is still generally ignored. Cluster- and network-oriented angles would be interesting though (for example, in the context of 'dominant firm clusters' or 'weak chains').

Rugman and Verbeke (1998) use the resource-based view to explain why companies do or do not make green investments. The use of the resource-based view in the environmental management literature was quite new at the time (since Hart, 1995) and is nowadays still accepted and widely used among scholars. It explains how companies can create firm-specific advantages by investing in green capabilities. The choice for this theory was not obvious at the time, but laid a basis for the further development of the resource-based view in the environmental management literature.

Reference

Hart, S.L. (1995). A natural-resource-based view of the firm. *Academy of Management Review*, **20**(4): 969–1014.

REVIEWS BY JONATAN PINKSE

Christmann, P. 2004. Multinational companies and the natural environment: Determinants of global environmental policy standardization. *Academy of Management Journal*, **47(5): 747–60.**

In her study, Christmann (2004) examines the influence of three external stakeholders – governments, industry participants and customers – on standardization of environmental management within multinational corporations (MNCs). The main aim of her study is to show how the nature of pressures exerted by different external stakeholders affects firms in their response to environmental challenges. She uses a mail survey for a sample of MNCs with US operations in the chemical industry. Her findings show that MNCs standardize different dimensions of environmental management in response to pressure from specific external stakeholders. MNCs that expected international harmonization of environmental regulations standardized environmental performance targets towards a global minimum; industry pressure led to standardization of operational environmental policies; and customer pressure led to standardization of the content of communications about environmental management practices.

Christmann also examines whether standardization of these three dimensions of environmental management depends upon functional strategies (e.g., research and development, production and marketing) and the dependence of an MNC on resources of a subsidiary. Results confirm that global standardization of all three dimensions is related to global standardization of functional strategies whereas subsidiary dependence affected global standardization of performance targets and operational policies, but not of communication.

Theoretically, the study is rather eclectic and does not adopt a clear theoretical perspective. Although she examines the influence of certain stakeholder groups on firms and cites some stakeholder literature, I would argue that she does not use insights from stakeholder theory per se. In fact, in developing her hypotheses she relies more on earlier empirical findings than theoretical logic. The only hypothesis that is rooted in theory is Hypothesis 2, which argues that industry pressure leads to environmental policy standardization in an MNC; firms try to enhance their legitimacy by copying successful competitors. This behavior is the main tenet from institutional theory, the process of isomorphism as put forward by DiMaggio and Powell (1983). So unlike Sharma and Henriques (2005), which is anchored in resource dependence theory, Christmann (2004) appears to use a kind of 'stakeholder theory' that is theoretically indebted to institutional theory. The main difference though is that the focus on institutional theory is not as apparent in Christmann (2004). Finally, it will come as no surprise that this study does not really contribute much to stakeholder theory; to be fair, this was not one of the aims in the first place. The main takeaway of Christmann (2004) is that she shows how MNCs deal with a complex global context in standardizing environmental policies.

References

DiMaggio, P.J. and Powell, W.W. 1983. The iron cage revisited: Institutional isomorphism and collective rationality in organizational fields. *American Sociological Review*, **48**(2): 147–60.
Sharma, S. and Henriques, I. 2005. Stakeholder influences on sustainability practices in the Canadian forest products industry. *Strategic Management Journal*, **26**(2): 159–80.

Eesley, C. and Lenox, M.J. 2006. Firm responses to secondary stakeholder action. *Strategic Management Journal*, 27(8): 765–81.

Eesley and Lenox (2006) conducted the only study of the three reviewed here that explicitly uses stakeholder theory and makes a contribution to this theory. The authors investigate when secondary stakeholders – those that do not have an economic stake in a firm, for example different kinds of non-governmental organizations (NGOs) – are able to elicit a positive response from firms regarding environmental issues. Theoretically, they build on one of the most-cited studies in the stakeholder literature, for example Mitchell et al. (1997). Mitchell et al. developed a model to identify which stakeholders are salient. This model contains two of the attributes seen in the two studies above, power and legitimacy (using insights from resource dependence theory and institutional theory), and adds 'urgency' as a third attribute.

The main contribution of Eesley and Lenox (2006) is that they do not just apply the Mitchell et al. (1997) model but advance it. Their main argument is that a stakeholder group's saliency in managers' minds is not a fixed attribute, but depends upon the specific request made. Moreover, firms are not alike, meaning that the same request from a stakeholder might elicit a positive response from one firm and a negative response from another. Eesley and Lenox, therefore, argue that it is the stakeholder–request–firm triplet that determines saliency. What this implies is that saliency is not determined by a manager of a certain stakeholder group, but instead by the actions of the group targeting the firm. In developing their hypotheses, the authors can now distinguish between stakeholder attributes and stakeholder request attributes.

Accordingly, they assert that power is a stakeholder group attribute; legitimacy can both be an attribute of a stakeholder group and the request made, and urgency is an attribute of a request not a stakeholder group.

To test their framework empirically, Eesley and Lenox (2006) collected data on actions by secondary stakeholder groups from the LexisNexis database. In operationalizing their main variables, the authors not only measure the power, legitimacy and urgency attributes, but also take the different tactics used by these stakeholders into account, for example proxy votes, civil suits, protests, boycotts and letter-writing campaigns. Their findings lend support to the assertion that there is a difference between group and request attributes, although not all their hypotheses are confirmed.

Notwithstanding the fact that this study tries to further develop stakeholder theory, it is still clear that stakeholder theory is highly ingrained in other organization theories. For example, Eesley and Lenox (2006) draw on resource dependency theory in conceptualizing the stakeholder–firm relationship. Nevertheless, their study is the only one that seems to really contribute to a stakeholder theory of the firm, if there is one.

Reference

Mitchell, R., Agle, B. and Wood, D. 1997. Toward a theory of stakeholder identification and salience: Defining the principle of who and what really counts. *Academy of Management Review*, **22**(4): 853–86.

Sharma, S. and Henriques, I. 2005. Stakeholder influences on sustainability practices in the Canadian forest products industry. *Strategic Management Journal*, 26(2): 159–80.

The main aim of Sharma and Henriques (2005) is to examine how different stakeholder influences affect firms' sustainability practices. As a theoretical framework, they use Frooman's (1999) model of stakeholder influence strategies that is anchored in resource-dependence theory (cf. Pfeffer and Salancik, 1978). Frooman suggested the dependence relation between a firm and a stakeholder – to what extent a firm relies on resources under the control of a stakeholder, or vice versa – determines how a stakeholder affects a firm. Sharma and Henriques (2005) particularly focus on one aspect of his model; that is, whether stakeholders employ a usage influence strategy or a withholding influence strategy. When a firm still has considerable control over its resources, stakeholders can only exert influence with a usage strategy, thus affecting how the firm makes use of its resources. When a firm has relatively less control, stakeholders have the option to withhold resources from a firm altogether.

To study stakeholder influences on sustainability practices empirically, the authors apply a content analysis on archival and survey data of a small sample of firms in the Canadian forestry industry. The authors found that

158 *Research companion to green international management studies*

environmental management practices that do not require fundamental change to the production process of a firm – pollution control and eco-efficiency measures – were not affected by stakeholder influences. More advanced practices that require substantial investments (e.g., eco-design, sustainable harvesting and use of alternative fibres) were brought about by different influence strategies used by different stakeholders. For example, investments in eco-design resulted from withholding strategies by environmental NGOs and usage strategies by customers and employees.

The main insight of the study is that the authors are able to find a relation between specific stakeholder influences and the implementation of certain sustainability practices. Moreover, the study not only takes account of stakeholder pressure, but also reckons that stakeholders can exert pressure in different ways, that is, withholding or usage strategies.

From an academic theory perspective, the study is an elegant application of the conceptual ideas of stakeholder theory put forward by Frooman (1999). However, the article has not much to contribute theoretically beyond showing empirical proof that the type of influence exerted by specific stakeholders matters for the implementation of sustainability practices. The reader learns more about under what conditions firms may implement more advanced sustainability practices rather than new insights related to Frooman's (1999) framework.

Surprisingly, this paper also suggests that there might not be such a thing called stakeholder theory. The main logic for a relationship between stakeholder influences and sustainability practices is derived from resource dependence theory. It is the power relation between the firm and its stakeholders that explains the degree of influence. Although this power relationship is a recurring theme in the stakeholder literature (cf. Hill and Jones, 1991; Mitchell et al., 1997), Sharma and Henriques rely almost exclusively on Frooman (1999).

In hindsight, I would have expected a more extensive analysis of the role of power and resources in the relation between a firm and its stakeholders. Nevertheless, the empirical contribution is important as the study goes beyond earlier work in showing that it is not just stakeholder pressure, but influence strategies that matter (a point also made by Eesley and Lenox, 2006).

References

Eesley, C. and Lenox, M.J. 2006. Firm responses to secondary stakeholder action. *Strategic Management Journal*, **27**(8): 765–81.
Frooman, J. 1999. Stakeholder influence strategies. *Academy of Management Review*, **24**(2): 191–205.
Hill, C.W.L. and Jones, T.M. 1992. Stakeholder-agency theory. *Journal of Management Studies*, **29**(2): 131–54.

Mitchell, R.K., Agle, B.R. and Wood, D.J. 1997. Toward a theory of stakeholder identi-fication and salience: Defining the principle of who and what really counts. *Academy of Management Review*, **22**(4): 853–86.

Pfeffer, J. and Salancik, G.R. 1978. *The External Control of Organizations. A Resource Dependence Perspective*. New York: Harper and Row.

REVIEWS BY SVENJA TAMS

Andersson, L. and T. Bateman. 2000. Individual environmental initiative: Championing natural environmental issues in U.S. business organizations. *Academy of Management Journal*, 43(4): 548–70.

Research question. The authors ask, what championing activities predict success of environmental championing episodes? More specifically, how does identification of environmental issues, their packaging and selling influence the following outcomes: (1) top management attention, (2) top management action, and (3) championing perception? Additionally, they ask whether the style of selling environmental issues moderated by the organizations' corporate environmental paradigm?

Intended contribution. The paper intends to provide a better understanding of the effectiveness of the *processes* used by environmental champions *within* organizational settings. Environmental champions are defined as individuals holding formal organizational roles and/or those involved in personal activism. This study seeks to extend literature on the personality characteristics and leadership qualities of individuals championing new products or technological innovations.

Theory. The research model and the hypotheses draw on a range of information processing, communications and influencing literature. Even though theoretical lenses are not accentuated, this paper draws conceptually on rational, symbolic and political perspectives on influencing. This approach enables the authors to formulate a set of alternative hypotheses and to offer interesting insights from their findings. For example, the authors find that emphasizing the financial opportunities of environmental initiatives is a significant predictor of success (and failure). But they also find that rational persuasion (the most frequently used influencing tactic) does not significantly predict success. In addition, they also find formal and businesslike rather than dramatic and emotional language as a contributor of success.

Methods. The study uses a survey of 132 environmental champions (27 percent of the initial sample) and semi-structured qualitative interviews with 22 champions, with 88 percent positioned within organizations with over 1000 employees. The description of the sampling method is very insightful, using leads through professional associations and snowballing of co-workers.

Strengths. Largely influenced by the approach taken by Dutton and Ashford (1993) on influencing and issue packaging, the authors develop a very comprehensive set of activities expected to influence the success of environmental championing. The authors articulate a wide range of

162   *Research companion to green international management studies*

alternative hypotheses that span rational, symbolic and political styles of packaging environmental issues.

With its focus on activities and practices associated with environmental championing, irrespective of formal level within the organization, this paper complements leader-centric approaches to green/sustainable change.

Another strength of the paper is that aside from a survey (n = 132, 27 percent of initial sample), the authors use qualitative interviews with a subsample to further inform statistical findings. This approach adds to the quality of their findings.

By using a survey design, the paper provides insights into the effectiveness of environmental championing tactics (success/failure as perceived by the champions).

Limitations. In 2009 (rather than the mid–late 1990s when the study was conducted), the authors' definition of what constitutes environmental management and their assumption that success of episodes is largely determined by organizational issues are limited.

For example, the authors identify a list of potential environmental issues (e.g., air pollution, waste disposal, wetlands destruction). This specific set and definition of environmental issues does not acknowledge the social construction of these issues or a more holistic/systemic approach of today's sustainability debate. For example, a complete product life cycle analysis may raise other issues, not previously considered. The latter perspective, central to contemporary sustainability management debates, is not reflected in the paper and would require a different approach to issue championing.

Another limitation of the paper is its organization-centric view of issue selling. This does not acknowledge the influence of wider institutional fields (societal change, consumerism, professionalization of green management, cross-sector collaboration, regulation, industry trends, competition, substitution, etc.).

The 'contained' definition of environmental champions does not consider the processes and practices related to more comprehensive leadership and change management, for example, directed at changing the environmental paradigm underpinning the culture and rationale of an organization. It also doesn't consider the role and influence of outside champions/change agents, in particular professional advisors and consultants. The authors acknowledge some of these limitations and the paper can be seen as a good starting point for a reframing of the research gap.

Practical relevance. The paper offers practical insights regarding the processes associated with innovation, issue selling and environmental championing. It is useful for management students and researchers conceptualizing further studies on related issues. Among several interesting findings the following stood out to me when reading this paper:

- Successful environmental championing requires a set of activities: identifying, packing (framing and presenting) and selling.
- Timing of influencing behaviors is important.
- Aside from communicating urgency and local impact of issues, the authors observe that 'the champions cited framing environmental issues in other ways – as simple, cutting-edge, relevant to corporate values, and good publicity – as reasons for the championing success' (Anderson and Bateman, 2000, p. 565). Moreover, 'framing an environmental issue as a financial opportunity may be one of the keys' (ibid.) to success.
- Championing environmental issues is like any other business issue and successful champions tended 'to downplay the "hotness" of their issues, instead relying on formal business language and familiar protocol' (ibid., p. 565).
- Aside from rational styles of communicating, political tactics such as coalition building and symbolic tactics invoking inspirational appeal were associated with success.
- A favorable organizational context matters in the influencing process.

Conclusions. Given the systematic conceptual and methodological design of this study, it offers a useful starting point for researchers interested in environmental management practices.

Reference

Dutton, J.E. and Ashford, S. 1993. Selling issues to top management. *Academy of Management Review*, **18**(3): 397–428.

Boiral, O., Cayer, M. and Baron, C.M. 2008. The action logics of environmental leadership: A developmental perspective. *Journal of Business Ethics*, 85: 479–99.

Research question. This conceptual article sets out to examine how differences in the enactment and effectiveness of environmental leadership can be explained. It addresses this question based on a distinction between organizational leaders' action logics associated with stages of consciousness development.

Intended contribution. The article promises insight into the relevance of developmental (i.e., cognitive constructivist) models of psychology as a foundation for explaining environmental leadership. The authors build on Rooke and Torbert's (2005) developmental model of leadership that distinguishes between seven action logics: opportunist, diplomat, expert, achiever, individualist, strategist and alchemist.

Boiral et al. (2008) observe several limitations in earlier literature. First, the authors recognize that the focus on environmental leaders' motives, vision and values is insufficient to explain effectiveness given the multi-layered systemic complexities inherent in environmental leadership. Moreover, managerialist approaches to environmental management are grounded in rational/instrumental assumptions of business while eco-centric perspectives tend to be 'too nonspecific to really elucidate the modes of thought and action of environmental leaders' (p. 482).

The authors use the notion of action logics because it is more comprehensive and integrated, considering the interconnection between leaders' perceptions (how they see), judgement (what they value), sensemaking (how they think), and behaviors (how they act). Boiral and colleagues argue (p. 480) that 'in addition to their personal ecological values, managers may have action logics that favor or, conversely, limit their capacity to exhibit committed, efficient, and adapted environmental leadership'. Specifically, distinguishing different types of action logics helps to differentiate between leaders' capacity for systemic thinking and integrating complex environmental problems.

Theory. The action logic model (Torbert, 2004) is grounded in constructivist-developmental theories (McCauley et al., 2006). This model is distinct from leadership perspectives that focus on interpersonal skills and the ability to mobilize others. In contrast, it emphasizes that individuals construct their reality (and leadership), that it is possible to identify different levels of consciousness, development and construction of reality, and that stages of consciousness development affect what individuals can become aware of, the way they construe reality and the way they act. Broadly, constructivist-developmental models distinguish between pre-conventional consciousness – characterized by impulsive and opportunist thinking, conventional consciousness – emphasizing efficacy within the context of established norms, and post-conventional consciousness – involving a reappraisal of accepted conventions, attention to complexity and interdependencies and interest in individual and societal transformation.

Applying the Rooke and Torbert (2005) model of action logics to environmental leadership (p. 488), the authors propose the following:

Pre-conventional

- *Opportunist logic* is characterized by little sensitivity to environmental issues except when they represent a threat or foreseeable gain for the manager; resistance to pressure from stakeholders, who are viewed as detrimental to economic interests; vision of the

environment as a collection of resources to exploit (DSP); and spo-
radic and short-term measures.

Conventional

- *Diplomat logic* supports environmental questions due to concern for appearances or to follow a trend in established social conventions; is concerned with soothing tensions related to environmental issues within the organization and in relations with stakeholders.
- *Expert logic* considers environmental issues from a technical, specialized perspective; reinforces expertise of environmental services; seeks scientific certitude before acting; prefers proven technical approaches.
- *Achiever logic* integrates environmental issues into organizational objectives and procedures; develops environmental committees integrating different services; responds to market concerns with respect to ecological issues; is concerned with improving performance.

Post-conventional

- *Individualist logic* is inclined to develop original and creative environmental solutions to question preconceived notions; develops a participative approach requiring greater employee involvement; and prefers more systemic and broader vision of issues.
- *Strategist logic* is inclined to propose a pro-environmental vision and culture for the organization, more in-depth transformation of in-house habits and values; development of a more proactive approach conducive to anticipating long-term trends; marked interest for global environmental issues; integration of economic, social and environmental aspects.
- *Alchemist logic* is directed at re-centering of the organization's mission and vocation with regard to social and environmental responsibilities; exhibits activist managerial commitment; involvement in various organizations and events promoting harmonious societal development; support for global humanitarian causes.

Discussion. The action logic model develops an understanding of the developmental and constructivist nature of leadership. In doing so, this article helps us to move beyond predicting environmental leadership based on discrete (and presumably stable) personality traits and behaviors as explanatory variables. It raises our awareness of the interdependencies of sets of cognitive and behavioral capacities. It also offers a more nuanced language for describing differences in the enactment of environmental leadership.

For example, the post-conventional logics of the individualist, strategist and alchemist recognize that leaders' ability to foster sustainable business involves the capacity to deal with systemic complexities. In contrast, the pre-conventional logic of the opportunist explains approaches to environmental management that are primarily economically driven. Conventional logics of the diplomat, expert and achiever explain different styles and methods of implementing environmental concerns within the organization.

I see the main benefit of this article as being in sharpening thinking and helping us to articulate the differences we observe in the enactment of environmental leadership. Enriching our vocabularies with the notions of the 'pre-conventional' opportunist, 'conventional' diplomat, expert and achiever, and 'post-conventional' individualist, strategist and alchemist enables sense-making with eloquence, elegance and confidence.

Having said the above, I see a central limitation of the paper in that the conceptual underpinnings of constructivist-developmental theory are not further examined. Perhaps an indicator of some of the conceptual limitations can be found in the authors' acknowledgement that 'relatively few in-depth studies have been conducted on managerial applications of these models' (p. 486). Quoting the percentages of people who Rooke and Torbert (2005) found to be associated with each stage appears out of context and seems to generalize from a sample about which no information is provided.

A further problem is that the action logic model distinguishes sharply between coherently integrated stages of consciousness. Even if statistical methods enable us to cluster (or factor analyse) people along distinct levels of consciousness and link these with different kinds of leadership behaviors, this does not confirm that individuals can be so neatly differentiated across distinct stages of consciousness. The authors do not challenge the assumption of Rooke (1997) that movement between stages 'represent[s] a sort of quantum leap' (Boiral et al., 2008, p. 493). Well, yes it may – or may not? It's certainly easier to spot quantum leaps. But what if human development unfolds, more often, along a continuous scale? How are we to notice, if we assume change to occur only in a quantum leap? Paradoxically, the assumption of coherent logics provides limited insights about human development that is of a more gradual, back-and-forth, context-dependent, chaotic and tentative nature.

Furthermore, the focus on individual leaders may ignore that environmental leadership is contextually embedded and socially constructed (Ospina and Sorenson, 2007). The dilemma of the strategist or alchemist leaders is that they are very likely to experience high systemic tension as result of at least 96 percent of their fellow human beings being characterized by a less advanced level of consciousness. I am intrigued by how they deal with the 'conventional' issues affecting their leadership task. Is there the possibility that an 'advanced' level of consciousness may be ineffective (i.e., 'aloof', 'remote', or 'isolated') because it is disconnected from organizational realities and fails to integrate vision back home? Rooke and Torbert (2005) acknowledge that strategists (4 percent) and alchemists (1 percent) are rare. But should we conclude from this, as seems to be implied, that they are always more effective leaders?

In sum, for those of us interested in advancing constructivist approaches to (environmental) leadership and its systematic development in organizational and educational settings, this article offers a clear overview of the issues.

I would recommend it to my students and invite discussion. The description of different stages of consciousness may be helpful when educating aspiring leaders and executives. Yet, the pedagogical usefulness of this model for particular groups needs to be carefully considered. I would expect this model to resonate well with students who are already exploring post-conventional approaches. It provides them with confidence and a sense-making model to explain why they feel at odds with more pre-conventional and conventional modes of environmental management. But I suspect it resonates less well with students who are still struggling to work out 'pre-conventional' and 'conventional' challenges in their development. In this case, educators could ask students to use the typology as a tool for the analysis of texts about environmental leadership.

As a researcher, this paper prompts me to consider carefully how we use existing conceptual models to inform our research. This paper should be the starting point for further research that examines critically the conceptual and methodological underpinning of constructivist approaches to leadership and for research that examines the connection between the psychological and collective construction of leadership and actual leadership behaviors and outcomes.

References

McCauley, C.D., Drath, W.H., Palus, C.J., O'Connor, P.M.G. and Baker, B.A. 2006. The use of constructive-developmental theory to advance the understanding of leadership. *The Leadership Quarterly*, **17**: 634–53.

Ospina, S. and Sorenson, G.L.J. 2007. A constructionist lens on leadership: Charting new territory. In G.R. Goethals (ed.), *The Quest for a General Theory of Leadership*. Cheltenham, UK and Northampton, MA, USA: Edward Elgar, pp. 188–204.

Rooke, D. 1997. Organizational transformation requires the presence of leaders who are strategist and magicians. *Organisations and People*, **4**(3): 16–23.
Rooke, D. and Torbert, R. 2005. Seven transformations of leadership, *Harvard Business Review*, **83**(4): 66–76.
Torbert, R. 2004. *Action Inquiry: The Secret of Timely and Transforming Leadership.* San Francisco: Berrett-Kohler.

Egri, C.P. and Herman, S. 2000. Leadership in the North American environmental sector: Values, leadership styles, and contexts of environmental leaders and their organizations. *Academy of Management Journal*, **43(4): 571–604.**

Research question. The authors offer three main research questions:

1. What are the differences between environmental and traditional leadership?
2. Is environmental leadership synonymous with transformational leadership (Bass, 1985)?
3. Do profit and non-profit environmental organizations conform to the theorized characteristics of ecocentric organizations (e.g., Gladwin et al., 1995; Shrivastava, 1995)?

   Intended contributions. The aim of the article is to examine the values, motives and unique qualities or skills of leaders in the North American environmental sector. It seeks to extend earlier research studying environmental leadership within case studies or particular environmental fields, by comparing individual aspects of environmental leadership across three types of organizations: (1) non-profit organizations dedicated to environmental concerns (including grassroots organizations and mainstream environmental organizations); (2) for-profit environmental organizations that commercialize environmentalism through products or services; and (3) 'mainstream' businesses.
   The article adds to our understanding of individual aspects of leadership and organizational design across two types of environmental settings. It broadens traditional notions of leadership, highlighting the role of ecocentric and related transformational values. It also suggests that strategic imperatives of organizations attract and facilitate the expression of such values (i.e., context matters).
   Theory. The article is grounded in an individualized view of environmental leadership. The values and beliefs associated with environmental leadership are assumed to be ecocentric (as opposed to expressing economic or technological concerns), based on a premise of interdependent inclusiveness, and is highly relational/transformational (as opposed to

power-based). Moreover, the study works from the assumption that the institutional context may attract leaders with such values and facilitate or constrain their expression.

The authors conceptualize environmental leadership as primarily an individually led activity that is (1) guided by a personal belief system (that deeply values and identifies with nature) and (2) enacts ecocentric values in organizational processes, activities and relationships. This individualist conceptualization is evident in their definition of environmental leadership as 'the ability to influence individuals and mobilize organizations to realize a vision of long-term ecological sustainability'. They further specify, 'Guided by ecocentric values and assumptions, environmental leaders seek to change economic and social systems that they perceive as currently and potentially threatening the health of the biophysical environment' (p. 572).

Methods. This is a comparative interview study conducted in 1995–96 in Canada and the US with 73 leaders of 38 for-profit green businesses and 22 non-profit environmental organizations.

A combination of qualitative and quantitative measures was used and examined through content and statistical analyses. Personal leader values of for-profit and non-profit environmental leaders were also compared with data from a sample of Canadian/US managers.

Findings. The study compares the occurrence of the following values across three institutional settings. Among its most significant findings, the reported study suggests:

- There are significant value differences between leaders in non-profit environmental organizations, for-profit environmental organizations and general manager samples.
- Non-profit environmental leaders have the strongest preferences for openness-to-change, self-transcendence, benevolence, universalism and ecocentric values.
- Transactional and transformational leadership were more strongly developed among leaders in the for-profit environmental sector than among those working in the non-profit environmental sector.
- Organizations in the non-profit environmental sector were characterized by more boundary-spanning task systems, adhocracy and network structures, and professional bureaucracy including clan modes of governance.
- Organizations in the for-profit environmental sector were characterized by more balance between technical core and boundary-spanning task systems, divisional and machine bureaucracy, and bureaucratic and market forms of governance.

Limitations. This article was clearly pioneering. Yet, from today's per-spective, we can also recognize some limitations.

Possibly as a reflection of the time at which the study was conducted (mid-1990s), the distinction between environmental non-profits, for-profits and traditional organizations appears rather monolithic. Each organiza-tional form is associated with a particular ideology/culture that can be expressed by a certain set of values and designs. This ignores heterogeneity within forms and the influence of wider institutional fields, in particular cross-sector interdependencies and field dynamics as a result of innovation and learning.

Some of the value dimensions examined are positioned along mutually exclusive/opposing scales. For example, openness to change is expected to be opposite to conservatism and self-enhancement is expected to be oppo-site to self-transcendence. As a result, it is difficult to discern whether these values are complementary. While this approach may have been justified within a world where sectors were considered to be relatively distinct and homogeneous, the emerging context of responsible and sustainable busi-ness and the rise of 'hybrid organizations' would call for greater consid-eration of leaders' ability to invoke complementary values and discourses (e.g., Maguire and Hardy, 2006). In particular, we may expect a greater heterogeneity of values within commercial organizations.

Based on Gladwin's (1993, p. 53) argument that a move to more sustain-able business requires 'fundamental transformations of mission, structure, and political, cultural, and technical systems', the authors set out to measure transformational leadership based on Bass's (1985) definition of transformational leadership. However, this operationalization of trans-formational leadership doesn't do justice to the scope of transformation called for by Gladwin.

Practical relevance. The findings provide a foundation for our under-standing of leadership in environmental organizations. From today's per-spective, we may expect that this relevance is limited by (1) an increasing transfer of business/results-oriented discourse into the non-profit sector and (2) a greater popularization of environmental concerns in mainstream business. The latter has created new opportunities for cross-sector collab-oration that require leaders' ability to connect across different discourses.

The article also contributes to our understanding of differences between more commercially oriented environmental organizations (e.g., social and sustainable enterprises in today's jargon) and more ideological-based movement and advocacy organizations.

Conclusions. The article represents one of the first systematic studies of environmental leadership and provides a good starting point for scholars interested in this topic. It is thorough in the sense of covering a wide range of values relevant to environmental leadership and organizational design of environmental organizations.

Today, its relevance appears limited as it does not give consideration to the complex and pluralistic context in which sustainable management is situated. This context requires leadership behaviors that bridge ideological and discursive divides and are transformational in a way that is not reflected in Bass's notion of transformational leadership (e.g. with its focus on the leader–follower relationship within organizational employment settings).

Moreover, environmental/sustainable leadership across wider organizational networks, or even fields, questions an individualized view of leadership (i.e., focusing on the leader) and calls for a view of leadership as a process of social construction (e.g., Foldy et al., 2008).

References

Bass. B.M. 1985. *Leadership and Performance Beyond Expectation*. New York: Free Press.

Foldy, E.G., Goldman, L. and Ospina, S. 2008. Sensegiving and the role of cognitive shifts in the work of leadership. *The Leadership Quarterly*, **19**(5): 514–29.

Gladwin, T.N. 1993. The meaning of greening: A plea for organizational theory. In K. Fischer and J. Schot (eds), *Environmental Strategies for Industry: International Perspectives on Research Needs and Policy Implications*. Washington, DC: Island Press, pp. 37–62.

Gladwin, T.N., Kennelly, J.J. and Krause. T.S. 1995. Shifting paradigms for sustainable development: Implications for management theory and research. *Academy of Management Review*, **20**(4): 874–907.

Maguire, S. and Hardy, C. 2006. The emergence of new global institutions: A discursive perspective. *Organization Studies*, **27**(1): 7–29.

Shrivastava. P. 1995. Ecocentric management for a risk society. *Academy of Management Review*, **20**(1): 118–37.

Index